R00337 35228

CHICAGO PUBLIC LIBRARY
HAROLD WASHINGTON LIBRARY CENTER

R0033735228

Y0-AZH-148

REF
LB
2844.2   Brock, Henry C.
.B76
1976   Parent volunteer
         programs in early
         childhood educa-
         tion

CHICAGO PUBLIC LIBRARY

FOR

REFERENCE USE

ONLY

NOT TO BE TAKEN FROM THIS ROOM

SOCIAL SCIENCES AND HISTORY DIVISION

Cop1

The Chicago Public Library

DEC 19 1977

Received

Parent Volunteer Programs

in Early Childhood Education

A Practical Guide

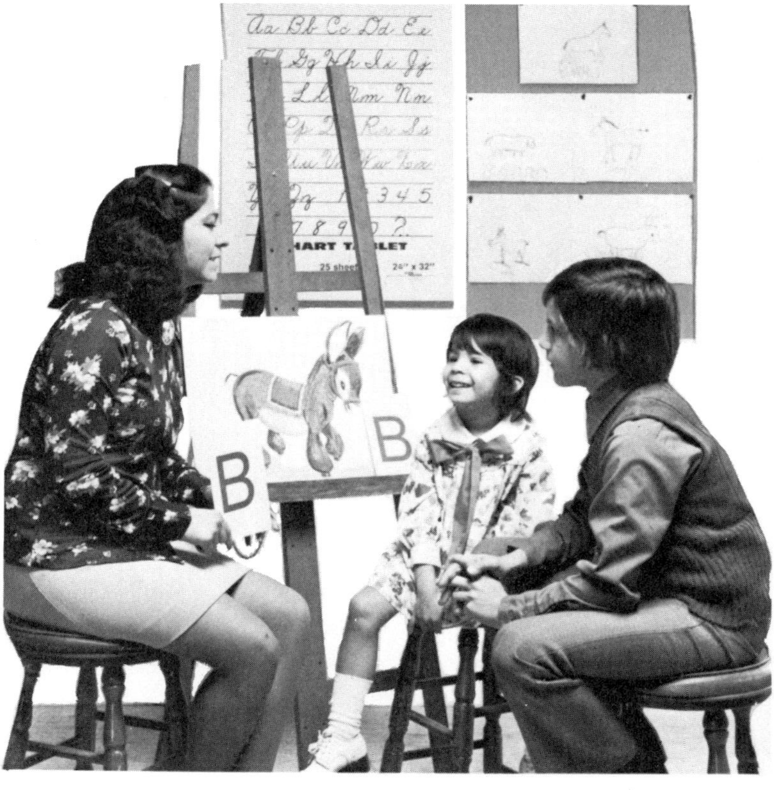
Aa Bb Cc Dd Ee
24" x 32"
B
B

Henry C. Brock III

A Practical Guide

Parent Volunteer Programs in Early Childhood Education

Linnet Books • 1976

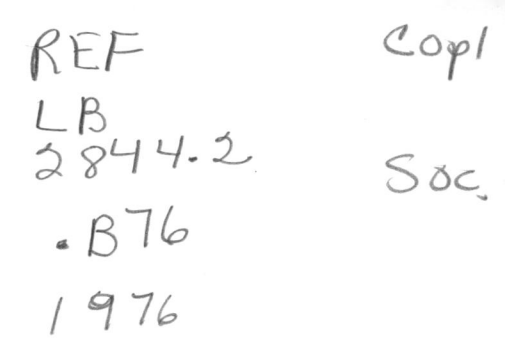

Library of Congress Cataloging in Publication Data

Brock, Henry C   1941-
Parent volunteer programs in early childhood education

  Bibliography: p.
  Includes index.
  1. Volunteer workers in education. I. Title.
LB2844.2.B76   372.1'1'412   76-8188
ISBN 0-208-01566-3

©The Shoe String Press, Inc., 1976
First published 1976 as a Linnet Book,
an imprint of The Shoe String Press, Inc.,
Hamden, Connecticut 06514

All rights reserved

Printed in the United States of America

Contents

Preface 9

Chapter I—Introduction......................... 11

    Pertinent Research • Federal Philosophy Regarding Parent Participation • The Need for Parent Volunteers • Legal Implications • Financial Considerations • Definition of Terms • Summary

Chapter II—Design Phase 23

    Introduction • Soliciting Suggestions • Selecting Goals and Objectives • Summary

Chapter III—Implementation Phase 35
    Introduction • Orienting the Staff • Obtaining a Parent Coordinator • Public Relations and Recruiting Volunteers • Screening and Placing Volunteers • Orienting and Training Parent Volunteers • Recognizing Volunteer Service

Chapter IV—Evaluation Phase 82
    Introduction • Evaluating Objectives • Conclusion

Notes 93

Appendixes 95
    A. Volunteer Organizations • B. Successful Programs

Sources Consulted 99

Index 111

Exhibits

Design Phase

Item 1. Staff Inquiry 31
2. Parent Inquiry—English 33
3. Parent Inqury—Spanish 34

Implementation Phase

Item 4. Orientation Information for Parent Volunteer
     Supervisors 56
5. Volunteer Attendance Record 59
6. Volunteer Information 60
7. Library Publications 61
8. Parent Coordinator Job Description 63
9. Information Leaflet—English 64
10. Information Leaflet—Spanish Translation 65
11. Volunteer Questionnaire 66
12. Library Assistant Job Description 68
13. Secretarial Assistant Job Description 69
14. Attendance Clerk Job Description 70
15. Grounds Supervisor Job Description 71
16. Health Assistant Job Description 72
17 Volunteer Record 73
18. Volunteer Record—Special Program and Activities
     Volunteers 74
19. Orientation for Parent Volunteers 75
20. Volunteer Self-Evaluation 79
21. Very Important Parent Award 81

Evaluation Phase

Item 22. Observed Results		87
23. Cover Letter		89
24. Student Handout		90
25. Evaluation Interview		91
26. Supervisor Evaluation of the Volunteer		92

Preface

Much has been written regarding the need for parent volunteer programs in early childhood education, but no complete, detailed program has been available. This book is being published to provide a *practical* resource for parents, teachers, librarians, and administrators— for all now involved, or considering becoming involved, in a parent volunteer program.

The most relevant information was drawn from an immense number of sources, examined, and sorted. In addition, over two thousand volunteer and staff manhours were spent under the direction of the author testing others' approaches as well as his own. Only those proved successful are included within these pages. Washington School (kindergarten through grade three) in the Selma (California) Unified School District was used by the author to field test the parent volunteer program during a two-year period. The model program described in chapters II, III, and IV is based on those experiences.

Throughout the book, in referring to the parent volunteer, the feminine gender is used because the majority of parent volunteers are women. It would be desirable to enlist more adult males for volunteer programs.

This book would not have been possible without the cooperation and help of many people. The parents of Washington School students and the parent volunteer supervisors at Washington School contributed many hours of time to the program. The parent coordinator, Mrs. Enedina Grijalva, the resource teacher, Mrs. Gwen Say, and the principal, Mr. Jack Pell, not only were extremely competent when implementing the model but also provided a great deal of encouragement and many practical suggestions.

Sincere gratitude is also extended to my friend, Dr. Rudolph H. Weyland, my parents, Mr. and Mrs. Henry C. Brock, Jr., and to my wonderful wife, Patricia, for their belief in the value of this work and many hours of dedicated assistance.

H.C.B.

CHAPTER I

Introduction

The early childhood years are widely recognized as the foundation for the manner in which the developing individual responds to his environment. This highly critical period helps determine how the child, and later the adult person, feels about himself, how he reacts to his family, peers, and education, and how ready he will be to learn.[1] The amount of parental involvement in the child's education may explain up to four times as much of the variance in the child's intelligence and achievement test scores at age eleven as is explained by the quality of the schools. Douglas, in a national sample of five thousand children in England, found that parent interest and involvement in a child's education were far more important than the quality of schools even after statistically allowing for family socioeconomic factors.[2]

Parent involvement in the classroom is an important element in early childhood education. It is mandated in many states for schools receiving early childhood education funds from state sources. When asked why parent volunteer programs are important, the California Superintendent of Public Instruction, Dr. Wilson Riles, replied, "The teacher needs to know all he can about the child and the parents need to know all they can about the school. Parents and teachers need to work together as a team."[3] An effectively designed, implemented, and evaluated parent volunteer program can accomplish improved student/school, family/school, and community/school relationships; improved adult/student ratio; and increased parent satisfaction, student motivation, as well as monetary savings.

The problems of our society, both social and economic, grow daily more acute, and possible solutions all point toward the necessity of making fuller and wiser use of all our human potentials and resources. Many of these solutions seem to call for the return of a greater share of responsibility for making institutions work to the people they are to serve through involvement in volunteer work for the common good. This is especially true of volunteer work by parents and other concerned citizens in the schools and other educational institutions, like libraries.

Of first importance are the educational benefits to the children. Parents and other community volunteers are likely to enrich and improve the learning process, since they are uniquely capable of tying the formal learning of the classroom and library-media center with the learning that goes on informally in the home and the community. Too, parent volunteer activity within the school is a prime antidote against the feelings of alienation from the professionals and what "they" are up to, that often today colors the feelings of people in all segments of society with regard to the schools.

Finally, in a period of economic stringency which seems likely to remain with us for some years to come, communities which want to maintain services may well have to turn to some old-fashioned community "in-kind" contributions of volunteer work to take the place of money that is not available. For all these reasons, there is already evidence of increasing involvement of parents in the day-to-day activities of the schools, and so it becomes ever more important that their contributions be coordinated and organized in the most effective way.

In this chapter, the research pertinent to the use of parents as volunteers in the education of their children, the federal philosophy regarding parent participation, the need for parent volunteers, legal implications, and financial considerations are discussed. Definitions of a few commonly used terms are also included.

Pertinent Research

Parent participation during the early childhood years is more important than participation at any other time in a child's education. Medical, psychological, and educational research have established that approximately eighty percent of a child's intelligence develops during the first seven or eight years of his life.[4] For this reason the preschool and primary grades are crucial to a student's later school success.

An important step in establishing a cooperative climate between a student's home and the school is recognition of the fact, supported by research, that the home and school can enhance a student's education by working cooperatively. Examples of some of the findings follow.

Moler, in a doctoral dissertation entitled "A Study of Good Parent Participation in Elementary Schools," makes the following general summary statements:

1. Parents contribute toward building good teacher morale.
2. Curricula are enriched by activities of parents.
3. Parents perform school publicity and public relations services.
4. Parents are active in promoting legislation and standards affecting schools and children.
5. Understanding children and providing for the social needs are important activities of parent participation.[5]

In a doctoral dissertation entitled "A Comparative Study of the Reading Achievement of Second Grade Pupils in Programs Characterized by a Contrasting Degree of Parent Participation," written at Indiana University by Ryan, the reading patterns of two groups were studied. The experimental group had a planned program of parent participation and the control group had only incidental parent participation. The summary of the major findings includes the following statements:

> The experimental group was significantly superior to the control group on the word meaning test. . . . Also, the study indicated the experimental group read more extensively, visited the library more frequently with parents and expected less help with new words from parents than did the control group.[6]

In his doctoral dissertation entitled "The Effect of Personal Contactual Relationships on Parents' Attitudes Towards Participation in Local School Affairs," Schiff indicates:

> Statistical evidence showed that personal contact

with school personnel by parents was effective in increasing parental acts of participation and cooperation....

Analysis of gains on the reading test revealed that pupils of the experimental group improved to a significantly greater degree than did pupils of the control group. Increased parent contacts were thus significantly effective in terms of pupil achievement gains in reading....

The data indicated that school attendance ... was significantly increased. The number and intensity of pupil behavior problems were reduced. Parental interest as measured by study habits was increased....[7]

Federal Philosophy Regarding Parent Participation

Congress, as evidenced by legislation enacted, believes parent participation is important in the education of youth. The Elementary and Secondary Education Act, Public Law 89-10, of April 11, 1965, Title I, was amended to require that local education officials involve parents. The Revised Criteria for Title I, also known as Program Guide Number 44, contains provisions specifically for the involvement of parents in Title I projects. Criterion 2.1 states: "The priority needs of educationally deprived children in the eligible attendance areas were determined in consultation with teachers, parents...." Criterion 5.4 indicates: "The Title I program includes appropriate activities or services in which parents will be involved."[8]

The regulations drawn up by the U. S. Office of Education for implementation of the Elementary and Secondary Education Act, Title I, clearly state that if payments are to be made to local educational agencies, parents are required to be involved in the planning, development, operation, and evaluation of Title I projects.[9] These requirements for parental involvement are considered minimal by the federal government. State education agencies may add additional requirements to ensure effective participation. Section 415 of the General Education Provisions Act, Public Law 91-230, states:

> In the case of any applicable program in which the Commissioner determines that parental participation at the state or local level would increase the effectiveness of the program in achieving its purposes, he shall promulgate regulations with respect to such program setting forth criteria designed to encourage such participation.[10]

As further evidence of federal belief in parent participation, another publication of the U.S. Department of Health, Education and Welfare, Office of Child Development, entitled *Project Head Start, Parent Involvement,* states:

> Parent involvement enables parents to participate (1) in making policy decisions that affect their children's growth and development and (2) in developing programs and assisting parents in carrying out their parental responsibilities based upon their desires and understanding.[11]

As has been shown, various research studies indicate the benefits of having parents involved in the education of their children. The philosophy of the federal government, as well as state and local governments, is increasingly encouraging parents to become active partners with school staff members in the education of their children.

The Need for Parent Volunteers

Parents may assist schools in many capacities. One popular area for parent volunteer service is the school library or media center. One young mother who had children in a Selma, California, school helped the librarian in the fall by placing checkout cards and pockets in the books which had arrived during the summer. She also stamped the school name inside the new books and typed the cards for the card catalog. During the entire school year, another mother helped with book repair and shelving, and a third parent assisted during the spring and summer with inventory, compiling overdue book lists, and fine collections.

Other parents assisted in helping the library become more than just a place to check out books and a "single culture" resource. The library blossomed into a multicultural center with parents setting up displays featuring African nations, Mexico, Japan, and other foreign countries. The librarian realized that parents want to feel that they can help and that it gives them great satisfaction to be a part of the educational system.

The potential benefit to students through the use of parent volunteers is especially great in schools and districts with large concentrations of minorities. It cannot be emphasized too much that the educational system is truly effective only if the community, through parent volunteer programs and other means, becomes involved in the educational process. Parent volunteers can work effectively too in agencies also devoted, though less formally than the school system perhaps, to early learning for young children, especially the public libraries.

One young, busy, Mexican American mother of two Washington School students contributed many volunteer hours when she was not working in the fields. She was invited by a teacher to a parent tea hosted by the staff in October, and she began working in her children's classrooms the following day. She started by assisting the teacher with the construction of visual aids and eventually assumed responsibility for working with individual students and small groups at reading and math centers. She indicated that she felt her participation had increased her children's motivation for learning and said, "I can see the difference at home as well as at school." [The statements made by parents and staff members were obtained during interviews conducted by the author.] The teacher in whose classroom this parent worked commented, "I don't know how in the world I would have gotten through all of the work without this volunteer's help."

Another parent assisted in the school office three days a week. Encouraged by the secretary, she had decided to volunteer on a regular basis, and indicated that she felt the time was well spent because her interest in the school had encouraged her third grade child to become more interested in his education. She assisted the secretary with the lunch count for the cafeteria, typing, and maintenance of attendance records. After working in the school office for a period of time, the volunteer commented, "For the first time in my life I feel at ease walking into a school."

Beside the improvement shown in student interest and achievement, the staff at Washington School felt the parent volunteers helped improve school/community relations. The resource teacher said, "They [the volunteers] serve as a pipeline to the community and make the school become alive and friendly to those less familiar with it."

Legal Implications

The legal implications of the use of parent volunteers vary widely throughout the United States, and in most cases the legal status of parent volunteers is not clearly defined by legislation or court decisions. It is important, however, that all parent volunteer program participants, parents, and staff alike be aware of the legal implications of being involved in a parent volunteer program. Information may be obtained from local site and district offices, county schools offices, state departments of education, and some professional organizations.

Frequently volunteers are not included under insurance policies and regulations covering staff members; thus their status should be defined prior to their participation in a program. In many districts they fall under the same insurance policies and regulations as "visitors."

Financial Considerations

Parent volunteers do not receive remuneration for the time they spend assisting the schools; nevertheless, a parent volunteer program is not "free." There are some costs involved, such as for materials, and if the program is large enough to warrant it, for staff to serve as administrators, coordinators, and secretaries.

As suggested earlier, there are state and federal compensatory education funds available to assist in developing and implementing volunteer programs. Program costs can also be underwritten by local citizen efforts, foundation grants, local funds, or by a combination of these.

In addition, there is the concept of "paid volunteers" which is being used successfully in many schools. In this type of program, volunteers are reimbursed for expenses incurred, such as meals, carfare, and babysitting. Strictly speaking, a participant cannot be considered a volunteer while receiving a salary. However, reimbursement of expenses gives additional incentive (indeed makes it possible in many poor neighborhoods) for parents to contribute time since it reduces or eliminates the financial obligations incurred as volunteers. Obviously no parent should be financially penalized for volunteering, and many willing helpers would be lost to the volunteer program if expenses incurred could not be reimbursed.

Parents may also be involved in determining how the funds for the parent volunteer program will be spent. An advisory committee composed of parent and school staff members may be used to administer the program including establishing a budget and authorizing expenditures. Of course, strict accountability should be required by the school employee responsible for the parent volunteer program.

Definition of Terms

Because this book is written for parents and other noneducators, as well as for professional educators, and librarians, professional terms have been replaced by more commonly used words and phrases; therefore, an extensive list of defined terms is not necessary. However, a few definitions are in order for some frequently used terms.

Individualized instruction allows students to progress through concepts at their own rate of speed. The teacher often gives a diagnostic test to determine what the student knows and what he needs to learn in a particular subject area. The results of this test indicate to the instructor which learning tasks need to be prescribed to assist the student in mastering the concept.

INTRODUCTION

As the student gives evidence that he has learned, he advances to the next learning challenge, geared by the teacher to his needs and abilities.

Parent participation is a broad term that includes any activity involving parents in the education of children. Parent participation may include membership on committees, helping students at home, or working at the school site.

A **parent volunteer** is any parent who is assisting at an educational institution on a voluntary basis. The parent volunteer need not necessarily have a child in the classroom in which she is assisting or at the school to which she is assigned. A parent volunteer receives no pay but may perform some of the same duties as a paid aide.

Program participants refer to both staff members and parents who participate in a parent volunteer program.

A **resource teacher** is a credentialed teacher assigned to be a "resource" to classroom teachers.

A **school parent volunteer program** is a framework that has been developed to provide persons to work as volunteers at schools under the direction of teachers and other school district employees in order to strengthen the school program and/or expand it through use of the volunteer's special knowledge and skills.

In this book the term **staff** is used to refer to all of the certified employees at a school site, including the principal, resource teacher, and all classified employees except the custodian.

The term **supervisor** is used here to refer to any school employee who has supervision responsibilities over one or more parent volunteers. Most of the supervisors are credentialed teachers or library-media specialists, but others may serve as supervisors of some volunteer activities.

Summary

This introductory chapter has dealt with a variety of topics pertinent to establishing a parent volunteer program. Knowledge of this background information may save time when a program is being developed. The remaining chapters provide information on how a program may be designed, implemented, and evaluated. In addition, a model program description with sample forms, handouts, and evaluation materials is included.

Any successful parent volunteer program must be constantly re-evaluated to remain successful. The information presented in these chapters describes how the program worked at one site. Policies and procedures which are effective and appropriate for one group of students, parents, and staff members one year may not be as satisfactory at other schools and in succeeding years. Each program at each site must be tailored to meet the needs of the individuals participating in it.

A review of the volunteer program at Washington School by the parents and staff at the end of the second year revealed the most important single aspect of the program was to create an environment which encouraged parents to become involved. The reception parents receive when they express an interest in serving as a volunteer must reflect warmth and a genuine interest in the volunteers as well as students.

It was also deemed important to create a team approach to working with children. A parent volunteer program should not become just another educational tool to be manipulated by the professionals. It is therefore beneficial to involve parents in all program phases including design and evaluation as well as implementation.

CHAPTER II

Design Phase

Introduction

Each parent volunteer program must be designed to fit the needs of the particular school and district in which it is to be implemented, and no two programs will be exactly alike. Chapter II describes the process of soliciting suggestions through the use of staff and parent inquiries (questionnaires) to assist with the design of a volunteer program. The selection of goals and specific measurable objectives is also presented here. For easy reference, each of the items mentioned in the model will be assigned an exhibit number and the page number on which it may be found will be included.

Soliciting Suggestions

Before the goals and objectives of a parent volunteer program are formulated, parents and staff members should have the opportunity to make suggestions for the program design. Ways to accomplish this include discussions between parents and staff members at meetings and during individual interviews, and the distribution of inquiries to both parents and staff members. The amount of support generated for the program is related to some degree to the involvement of parents and staff members in the initial planning stages.

Staff Inquiry. The purposes of the staff inquiry [Item 1 of page 31] used at Washington School were to (1) obtain staff suggestions for program goals, (2) determine what duties volunteer supervisors might assign to parents, and (3) determine what suggestions the staff had regarding what aides, teachers, and administrators could do to encourage parents to volunteer.

The inquiries were given to staff members during private interviews held with the principal early in the school year. The purposes of the interview were to inform each teacher and aide about the parent volunteer program, distribute the staff inquiry, and solicit support and suggestions for the program design and implementation.

In answer to the request for staff suggestions regarding the goals of the program, all the respondents felt that the development of better working relationships among home, community, and school should be a principal goal of the program. Other goals frequently mentioned were: to provide individual instruction for Washington School students; to provide enrichment lessons or activities for students; to provide instruction in English for non-English-speaking students through the

DESIGN PHASE

use of bilingual volunteers; and to increase children's motivation to learn. The most frequently mentioned duties volunteer supervisors might assign to parents, both inside and outside the classroom, included correcting papers and recording grades, typing and duplicating materials, working with individuals and small groups, and constructing learning materials.

The school library-media center is another learning site frequently mentioned by the staff in which parent volunteers can be of tremendous help in a variety of ways. In addition to routine paperwork tasks in connection with ordering, organizing, and repairing books and audiovisual materials—such as typing, filing, pasting, and reshelving—parent volunteers can take an effective and active role in one-to-one and group activities with children. These include story telling, tape recording of original stories, reading aloud, using film strips, helping to arrange slides for a pupil created slide presentation, assisting with independent learning projects, tutoring, and dozens more.

Assistance to nonteaching support staff such as the school nurse or the school secretary was also mentioned as a possible duty for parent volunteers; lunchroom and playground duty and help to teachers and other school staff on field trips were also cited as possible volunteer activities.

Various ways were suggested by aides, teachers, and administrators to encourage parents to volunteer. Personal interaction was most frequently mentioned; staff members could meet with parents in their homes, or by telephone, or in general meetings and explain the responsibilities and rewards of being volunteers. It was felt most important, however, to make parents feel welcome when they volunteered. For volunteers to feel time is well spent, useful tasks are essential.

Parent Inquiry. The parent inquiry (Item 2, page 33) was designed by the author and then evaluated by three teachers, three principals, and three parents. The comments of the nine evaluators were taken into consideration and revisions in the inquiry were made. The inquiry was then evaluated by three additional parents and further revisions were made.

The inquiry was printed in English, but because of the substantial number of Spanish surnamed families in the school attendance area, a Spanish translation was printed on the reverse (Item 3, page 34). The inquiries were distributed and explained at a faculty meeting and then sent home with each child at the end of the next school day. A candy reward was given to each student when an inquiry was returned to Washington School. There was a return rate of eighty-three percent.

The first purpose of the inquiry was to determine the extent of the parents' willingness to serve in the parent volunteer program. The names of those who indicated an interest were recorded for future reference.

The second purpose was to gather information regarding potential problems affecting parents' decisions to volunteer. A large portion of the respondents indicated that child care responsibilities would not allow them to participate; some said they were working; others had health problems; some were attending school; and a few indicated that language limitations made them apprehensive. The situations regarding employment, health problems, and education were unalterable by the staff at Washington School; but it was determined that parent participation could be increased by providing child care for volunteers and by providing activities or tasks which would not require a command of the English language, such as sewing costumes for school activities.

The third purpose of the inquiry was to get parents'

DESIGN PHASE

suggestions as to how the staff might make it easy for the parents to volunteer. Parents stressed the importance of being notified well in advance of when their services were needed to allow them time to make plans.

Selecting Goals and Objectives

Goals and objectives must be tailored for each volunteer program at each school and may vary from year to year. It cannot be overemphasized that parents as well as staff members should be involved in determining the direction of each program. The "goal" of a program is a *broad* description of what the program is to accomplish, usually over the period of one school year. An "objective" of a program is a *specific* statement of a step toward the goal to be accomplished and it must in some way be measurable. Examples of both goals and specific measurable objectives follow.

At Washington School, the selection of goals and objectives for the parent volunteer program was a joint effort involving parents and staff members. The goals recommended by the principal, teachers, and aides on the staff inquiry were discussed with members of the Washington School Parent Teachers Association and approved by them. Then a specific measurable objective was jointly developed for each goal. Without the measurable objectives, it would have been difficult to determine if the goals had been reached.

Various forms were used to record data to determine whether or not the objectives had been met: (1) A Volunteer Information sheet completed for each volunteer by the supervisor (chapter III, Item 6, page 60); (2) the Observed Results evaluation instrument completed by parents and staff members (chapter IV, Item 22, page 87); and (3) a Student Handout distributed to students (chapter IV, Item 24, page 90).

A rating scale was used in those objectives requiring evaluation by parents and staff members. The scale ranged from a high of seven to a low of zero. Gradations of values between four and seven indicated success, and values below four indicated varying degrees of less than successful ratings.

The following goals and objectives were established for the school year:

1. Goal: The parent volunteer program will strengthen home/community-school relations.

    a. *Objective:* When staff members and parents are asked the question, "Did the program strengthen home/community-school relations?" a minimum mean value of four on a scale of seven will be obtained.

Because of their associations with parents and other members of the community, the teachers, aides, and participating parents were asked to evaluate the program with respect to the objective of improving home/community-school relations.

    b. *Objective:* During the school year fifty parents will participate in the parent volunteer program.

Home/community-school relations may be improved by increasing the number of parents working at the school and becoming familiar with the school program.

2. Goal: Parent volunteers will provide individual instruction for Washington School students.

    a. *Objective:* Twenty-five percent of the students will receive two or more hours of individual instruction from a parent volunteer.

Since the length of individual instruction might vary from less than a minute to an indefinite number of hours, it was necessary to indicate a measurable amount of time spent with each student, although not necessarily all during one lesson. The two-hour figure was used because it was felt by those providing suggestions for goal and objective design that this span of time might allow a parent to establish rapport with a student and provide in-depth skill instruction.

3. Goal: Parent volunteers will provide enrichment lessons or activities for students.
    a. *Objective:* Twenty-five percent of the students will receive an enrichment lesson or activity presented by a parent.
    Enrichment lessons or activities were defined as experiences provided by volunteers which broadened student understanding of teacher introduced topics.

4. Goal: Bilingual parent volunteers will provide instruction in English for non-English-speaking students.
    a. *Objective:* Fifty percent of the non-English speaking students will receive two or more hours of individual instruction in English from a Spanish speaking volunteer.

5. Goal: The program will increase children's motivation for learning.
    a. *Objective:* When students are read the question "How do you feel about having someone else's parent help you here at school?" a greater number will respond by selecting a happy face than a neutral or unhappy face on a handout provided by the teacher.
    b. *Objective:* When staff members and parents are asked the question "Did the use of parent volunteers increase the children's motivation for learning?" a minimum mean value of four on a scale of seven will be obtained.

6. Goal: Program participants will judge each compo-

nent of the parent volunteer program successful.

    a. *Objective:* When staff members and parents are asked to rate each component of the parent volunteer program, a minimum mean assigned value of four on a scale of seven will be obtained.

Summary

This chapter has described the method of involving parents and staff members in the design of a parent volunteer program through the use of inquiries and assisting in the formulation of goals and objectives as carried out by the author at a particular school. In the light of that experience other goals, with other measurable steps toward their achievement might have been selected, but these served that particular situation well as a beginning framework. Perhaps the most important thing to remember in setting up a goals and objectives design is that they must be constantly re-evaluated and refined as one gets into the program.

[ITEM 1. STAFF INQUIRY]

WASHINGTON SCHOOL
Selma, California 93662

Dear Colleague:
　　The purpose of this inquiry is to gain information regarding a parent volunteer program for Washington School and it will take only a few minutes to complete. Your answers will, of course, remain confidential. Please return this to the resource teacher at your earliest convenience.
　　Thank you for your assistance.

1. What duties that would be helpful to you can a parent volunteer perform in the classroom?

2. What duties that would be helpful to you can a parent volunteer perform outside the classroom?

3. What can aides do to encourage parents to volunteer?

[ITEM 1, Continued]

4. What can teachers do to encourage parents to volunteer?

5. What can administrators do to encourage parents to volunteer?

6. Please list five goals you would like to see the program accomplish.

    1.
    2.
    3.
    4.
    5.

Additional comments regarding a parent volunteer program may be placed here.

Check one:

_____   _____   _____
 aide   teacher   Signature

[ITEM 2. PARENT INQUIRY - ENGLISH]

WASHINGTON SCHOOL
Selma, California 93662

Dear Parent:

The purpose of this inquiry is to determine how you feel about volunteering to help the students at Washington School. The staff is starting a parent volunteer program and your response to the questions below will provide valuable information. The questionnaire will take only a few minutes to complete. If you indicate that you are willing to volunteer, please sign your name in the space provided at the end of the inquiry. Your signature will allow us to contact you in the future to provide additional information regarding the program. Your answers will, of course, remain anonymous, if you choose not to sign. Please place the inquiry in the enclosed envelope and send it to school with your child by this Friday.

Thank you for your assistance.

Sincerely,

Mrs. Gwen Say   Mr. Jack Pell
Resource Teacher   Principal

1. Would you be willing to help at your child's school this school year? (Check one)
   Yes ____ No ____ Maybe ____
1a. If you answered "no", please describe why you would not be willing to participate.
1b. If you checked "maybe" on question 1, please indicate under what conditions you would be willing to help at your child's school.
2. What may the schools do to make it easier for you to volunteer?
3. Additional comments may be placed here.

Signature (optional)   Address   Phone No.

[ITEM 3. PARENT INQUIRY - SPANISH]

Estimados Padres:
El proposito de este cuestionario es para averiguar sus ideas en cuanto a un programa de padres voluntarios para ayudar a los alumnos de Washington School. Los directores y los maestros estan empezando un programa de padres voluntarios y sus respeustas en el cuestionario nos proveeran con informacion importante y esto solo tardara unos minutos. Si usted indica que quiere ser voluntario o voluntaria, haga el favor de firmar su nombre en el espacio al final de cuestionario. Su firma nos ayudara a communicarnos con usted en el futuro para darle mas informacion en cuanto al programa. Por supuesto, sus respeustas quedaran anonimas si prefiere no firmar el cuestionario. Meta el cuestionario en el sobre que le mandamos y mendelo a la escuela con su hijo antes del fue de semana.

                Sinceramente,

        Mrs. Gwen Say   Mr. Jack Pell
        Resource Teacher   Principal

1. Estaria dispuesto (o dispuesta) a ayudar en la escuela de su hijo (o hija) este ano escolar? (Escoja uno)
   Si____ No____ Quizas ____
1a. Si usted ha contestado que "no", explique por que no estaria dispuesto (o dispuesta) a participar.
1b. Si usted ha indicado "quizas" a cuestion 1, explique con que condiciones estaria dispuesto (o dispuesta) a participar en la escuela de su hijo o hija.
2. Que podrian hacer las escuelas para facilitarles a ustedes a ser voluntarios?
3. Otros comentarios pueden ser escritos aqui.

_____ _____ _____
Firma (no es necessaria)   Direccion   No. de
                                                                 telefono

CHAPTER III
Implementation Phase

Introduction

In his last speech before leaving for Texas, President John Kennedy remarked that, in education, "Things don't just happen; they are made to happen."[12] The general aim of the parent volunteer program implemented at Washington School in Selma, California, was to develop a cooperative partnership between parents and the school for the benefit of students.

Six goals had been outlined by solicitation of opinion from both the staff and parents and through joint discussion and effort. Now the time had come to identify the activities basic to implementing the parent volunteer program. They were defined as follows:

1. Orienting the staff of the school to the rationale and utilization of parent volunteers;
2. Writing a job description for, and selecting, a parent volunteer coordinator;
3. Preparing a public information program about the volunteer program, and recruiting volunteers;
4. Screening volunteer applicants and selecting those with the necessary qualifications;
5. Assessing placement opportunities and training volunteers;
6. Recognizing volunteer services, thus preventing drop-outs and reinforcing commitment;
7. Continuing evaluation of goals, methods, procedures, and materials and the effectiveness of the program overall.

Orienting the Staff

Most administrators, and other educators for that matter, recognize the need to provide at least some minimal amount of training to volunteers before they may be expected to perform efficiently as part of the school's program. Less well recognized is the need to orient teachers and other staff members to the proper roles and expectations for the volunteers and for themselves in relationship to the volunteers. The orientation and training of staff members so that they utilize parent volunteers effectively is as important as the orientation and training of the volunteers themselves.

A guidebook or manual designed for teachers, librarians, and other staff members may be used to summarize information about the program such as goals,

IMPLEMENTATION PHASE

objectives, policies and procedures, and other pertinent facts. It should, however, be used in addition to, and in reinforcement of, a staff development workshop at which concerns and attitude adjustments may be aired and discussed, and questions answered.

Relationships between staff members and parent volunteers should be very thoroughly understood and clearly spelled out. It is important that teachers and other staff members be reassured that the volunteers are there to support and assist them, to extend their efforts and enable them to perform better the most professional aspects of their work such as planning, individualizing student instruction, and evaluating student performance. A parent volunteer program can be substantially hurt, put off course, if there is any word in circulation, or any thought, even, that teachers or other staff might or could be replaced by the volunteers.

At Washington School, staff members were initially informed of the parent volunteer program when they were interviewed, and through distribution of the staff inquiries by the principal prior to the start of planning the program. A staff meeting was held to further orient the teachers and aides, each of whom was provided with a copy of the goals and objectives and a handout (pamphlet) entitled *Orientation Information for Parent Volunteer Supervisors* (Item 4, page 56). This pamphlet discussed the orientation and training the volunteers would receive, gave hints for getting off to the right start with volunteers, suggested ways of establishing confidence in parents, etc.

Each parent volunteer supervisor was asked to record the hours each volunteer spent under his supervision on the Volunteer Attendance Record (Item 5, page 59). Each supervisor was also asked to maintain records adequate to complete at the end of the year a Volunteer Information sheet (Item 6, page 60) for each parent. The data gathered from this form were used to determine whether or not the objectives had been met.

Each staff member was also made aware of materials relating to parent volunteer programs available in the school library-media center. A list of the publications in the library (Item 7, page 61) was distributed to those in attendance.

Obtaining a Parent Coordinator

A parent coordinator is needed to take responsibility for administering, designing, implementing, and evaluating a parent volunteer program. A well-organized, effective program requires a leader with the time and talent to devote to the project. The coordinator requires administrative skill, enthusiasm, flexibility, and the ability to communicate and relate well to others.

The coordinator of a parent volunteer program should be a person employed by the school district on a part-time or a full-time basis for that position. It may be someone who is already employed by the school district who is reassigned and designated coordinator for the program. A staff coordinator might be a teacher, administrator, guidance counselor, or reading specialist, but she should be relieved of some of her workload to take on the job. The coordinator may be a parent volunteer instead of an employee of the district, but in most cases this does not provide for proper authority or necessary checks and balances and is not satisfactory or recommended. However, it may work in the case of a single school building.

The coordinator may work with one particular school, a group of schools, or an entire school district. Her tasks will depend upon the needs of the district or the school, the types of professional and parental assis-

IMPLEMENTATION PHASE

tance available, and the availability of funds. The following duties may be assigned to a parent coordinator:

1. Initiate the process required to establish goals for the program.
2. Assist with the design of the program by providing staff work and a clearinghouse for all inputs.
3. Draft and supervise planning and operations in recruitment of volunteers.
4. Orient and train volunteers and assist the administration in orientation of teachers.
5. Order supplies and materials with inputs from media specialists (librarians) and concerned teachers and other staff.
6. Maintain volunteer records.
7. Contact and deal with volunteer parents with irregular attendance or unsatisfactory performance.
8. Plan with administration to recognize volunteer service.
9. Assist with evaluating the program.

For the model program at Washington School, a job description (Item 8, page 63) and a list of qualifications for the position of Parent Coordinator were prepared by the principal. The qualifications included: (1) ability to relate well to children and other adults, (2) previous experience as a parent volunteer, (3) ample time to devote to the program, and (4) enthusiasm for public education in general and the particular parent volunteer program.

The names of potential candidates for the position of parent coordinator were solicited from the teachers and aides. The list compiled from staff members' suggestions was then reviewed by a committee composed of the principal, parents, teachers, and aides. Five parents were selected as candidates for the position and asked if they would consent to an interview. The purposes of the interview were to (1) provide a detailed explanation of expectations for the parent volunteer program, (2) discuss the duties of the parent coordinator, and (3) evaluate the candidate's qualifications.

The principal discussed the details of the parent volunteer program and the coordinator's job description with each candidate. Each was informed that the coordinator would be responsible to the principal and to the resource teacher. The coordinator's duties included overseeing the entire program, recruiting parents, maintaining records, and encouraging volunteers to attend regularly.

The candidate selected was the school secretary who volunteered time beyond her hours of employment to be the parent coordinator. She indicated that she would be able to devote ample time to the position and demonstrated enthusiasm for the program and expressed belief that "This is one way we can really help our children." Her ability to relate to students and develop rapport with adults was evidenced by her past experience and record. She said that she enjoyed working with parents and children and that she wanted to help improve the quality of education at Washington School. She had three children in the Selma schools and one of these, a six-year-old, was a student at Washington. This arrangement worked well because she was familiar with the school and was closely supervised by the resource teacher and principal.

Public Relations and Recruiting Volunteers

According to Project VOICE's *How-To-Do Handbook*, a public relations program has two purposes: "One is to keep the volunteers informed about and

IMPLEMENTATION PHASE

interested in their own activities. The other is to provide the community with facts that make for an improved image for the school through its volunteer services."[13]

Public relations programs require not only that the community be informed initially of the program but also that it be kept aware of the services the volunteers provide. Information can be disseminated effectively through the use of television, radio, newspapers, magazines, and brochures. An open house may also be helpful in providing the community with information regarding the parent volunteer program.

One obvious objective of the public relations component is to recruit and retain as many volunteers as necessary for the program to function at its optimum level. The administrators in each school and district must determine which methods are most appropriate for their particular situation. As suggested above, the following approaches are some that may be used:

1. Send questionnaires, brochures, and/or flyers to parents.
2. Speak and work with PTA's and other organizations. Form a Speaker's Bureau consisting of people who are representatives of the population to be reached.
3. Distribute posters and use marquees.
4. Prepare articles and programs for newspapers, radio, and television to inform the community of the school needs and the contributions parents can make.
5. Ask staff members to identify potential volunteers.
6. Encourage satisfied volunteers to tell their friends about the program.
7. Telephone potential volunteers and invite them to coffee klatches at school or in homes.
8. Contact parents with prior school experience, for example, parents with experience in the Head Start Program.

9. Arrange tours of the school sites and open houses which will give people a firsthand view of the program.

10. Arrange parent education classes that are designed to give parents self-confidence and generate interest.

11. Consult volunteer bureaus.

12. Be friendly to, and show an interest in, parents and their views.

Examples from the Washington School experience follow.

Information Leaflet. Each of the students at Washington School was given an informational leaflet and asked to take it home to his parents. This announcement was prepared in English (Item 9, page 64) but with a Spanish translation on the reverse (Item 10, page 65).

Newspaper Article. An interview was held with a reporter of a local newspaper and an article appeared in the paper which briefly described the program and encouraged parents to telephone Washington School for further information. The article read as follows:

> Selma's Washington School is seeking parental participation in a parent volunteer program.
> School officials said they are encouraging parents to volunteer to help in classrooms, the library, the office, or on playgrounds.
> "The only qualifications are a genuine interest in young children and dependability," officials at the school said.
> There is no limit on the amount of time parents may volunteer to spend.
> More information may be obtained by calling Washington School, 896-3415.[14]

IMPLEMENTATION PHASE

Radio Announcement. An announcement briefly describing the parent volunteer program and requesting volunteers was sent to radio stations in the Selma listening area. The announcement stated:

> Washington School in the Selma Unified School District is inviting all parents of Washington students to participate in a Parent Volunteer Program. Parents may volunteer to help in the classroom, library, office, or on the school playgrounds. The only qualifications are a genuine interest in young children and dependability. Parents may volunteer as much or as little time as they wish. Anyone interested in further information may call Washington School, 896-3415.

Parent Tea. A parent tea was planned by the staff for the purposes of providing an opportunity for parents to talk with staff members regarding their children, providing staff members and parents the opportunity to become better acquainted, providing parents with information regarding the need for parent volunteers, and encouraging parents to volunteer their time.

The names of potential parent volunteers for an invitation mailing list were obtained from staff recommendations and returned parent inquiries. The invitations were personalized and contained the parent's name and date, time, and location of the tea. Telephone calls were also made by the parent coordinator to all parents to remind them of the event. The tea was held from 2:00 until 4:00 P.M. in the Washington School library during October.

Name tags were distributed to each parent upon arrival, and staff members also wore name tags. All of the tags were color coded. Each class was assigned a color; the name tags for the teacher, aide, and parents of students assigned to a particular classroom were constructed from paper of that color. This technique allowed parents to recognize more easily their child's teacher and aide.

Since it was anticipated that not all parents would arrive at the same time, refreshments were served before the staff presentations. Parents were then seated in small groups of six to encourage interaction.

The program included the following speakers and topics:

    I. Principal.
       A. Welcome.
       B. Introduction of staff members.
   II. Resource Teacher.
       A. Explanation of name tags.
       B. Description of the purposes of the program.
       C. Explanation of how parents were chosen to receive invitations.

Each parent present was asked to indicate what volunteer activities would interest her, what hours and days she could participate, and where she could be reached. After the tea, this information was forwarded to the appropriate teacher.

Comments from the resource teacher following the tea included: "Parents stayed longer than I thought they would" and "They seemed to have fun and enjoy themselves."

Screening and Placing Volunteers

Many methods are available for screening and placing or assigning volunteers. However, most school staff members and parent coordinators agree that volunteers should only be placed in positions in which staff members have requested volunteer services; requiring any

IMPLEMENTATION PHASE

school employee to accept a parent volunteer may do more harm than good.

Volunteers may be screened by interview, or by written application, or by a combination of both methods. Suggested qualifications which may reveal themselves in the application form and interview are:

1. The ability to relate to children, to be interested in them, and to accept them as individuals.
2. Willingness to give of themselves freely.
3. The time and the discipline to meet volunteer commitments on a regular basis.
4. Enthusiasm about education.
5. Good health and moral character.
6. The ability to work under supervision and to follow instructions.

The needs of the program must be matched with the abilities, time, and personalities of the volunteers. Experience indicates that the volunteers who have been placed according to their interests and abilities will provide regular service over a longer period of time than those who have not been so carefully placed.

Volunteers who seem unable to establish rapport (after a reasonable period for overcoming shyness and gaining confidence) with the students should be transferred to work that requires infrequent student contact. For instance, they may be able to assist the staff in such ways as making costumes and constructing visual aids. If others find it difficult to adjust to working at the school site, there are some jobs which can be done at home.

Thus there are many different ways in which volunteers may be utilized to improve the instructional program of a school or district. Each volunteer brings unique interests and abilities to the school site, and these particular qualifications should be taken into consideration when the volunteer is placed and duties are assigned.

Responsibilities designated for volunteers may include those in various categories. Two major fields of interest are helping in the classroom and library-media program. Instructional duties may include:

1. Tutoring students on a one-to-one basis,
2. Working with small groups of students,
3. Working with large student groups,
4. Working with students who speak English as a second language,
5. Assisting the administration of diagnostic tests,
6. Passing out and collecting materials,
7. Assisting with recreational and learning games,
8. Helping students with reference work,
9. Assisting in clarifying directions,
10. Correcting papers,
11. Helping record attendance and grades,
12. Assisting with room decorations, including bulletin boards and exhibits,
13. Cleaning up, including securing and putting away classroom supplies,
14. Preparing audiovisual aids and operating audiovisual equipment,
15. Helping to construct learning aids,
16. Assisting students with makeup work,
17. Reading to children and storytelling,
18. Listening to students read,
19. Taking color slides and preparing them for curriculum related use,
20. Arranging and maintaining a picture file.

Clerical-technical duties in the media center specifically might include:

IMPLEMENTATION PHASE

1. Placing check-out cards and pockets in new books,
2. Stamping school identification in new books,
3. Typing cards for the card catalog,
4. Repairing books, mending AV materials,
5. Compiling overdue book lists,
6. Shelving books,
7. Taking inventory,
8. Checking out books to students,
9. Collecting fines,
10. Setting up displays.

Of course, volunteers can help in numerous other areas, from clerical to supervisory, and including special activities both within and outside the school. Some other ways volunteers can help are:

1. Translating for parent conferences and translating notices to be sent home,
2. Assisting in dealing with attendance problems by record keeping, telephoning, and making home calls,
3. Assisting with the operation of the health office,
4. Typing and duplicating instructional materials,
5. Helping with office inventories,
6. Collecting lunch money and taking the lunch count, and/or supervising the lunchroom during the noon period,
7. Supervising playground activities before school, during breaks, and after school;
8. Supervising the halls and restrooms before school, during breaks, and after school, and
9. Supervising the loading and unloading of school buses.

Special programs and activities take advantage of particular volunteer talents. For instance, those with special areas of interest and expertise may speak to classes. Others may assist with field trips or act as a liaison between the school staff and other parents and community members.

Other special activities include:

1. Assisting with setting up displays in offices and corridors,
2. Helping with plays and skits,
3. Accompanying on piano or giving other instrumental or vocal music lessons and demonstrating either vocally or instrumentally,
4. Providing assistance with repair of school facilities,
5. Providing improved communication between the teacher and parents through home visits.

At Washington School, staff members were asked to notify the parent coordinator whenever they became aware of a parent who wished to become a participant in the parent volunteer program. The parent coordinator contacted the potential volunteer and suggested that she complete a Volunteer Questionnaire (Item 11, page 66). The questionnaire provides a record of the following information: name of volunteer, address, telephone number, names of children attending Washington School, health information, emergency information, work experience, and ability to speak and/or write Spanish. [In another area another language might be helpful.] A file was initiated by the parent coordinator for each parent and the volunteer questionnaire was placed in it.

Potential volunteers were interviewed by the parent coordinator prior to assignment to a supervisor. The application was discussed, and each was asked if she had specific placement requests. If so, the appropriate supervisor was contacted and an interview with the

IMPLEMENTATION PHASE

parent was arranged. If they agreed to work together, the parent was placed with that supervisor.

Various job descriptions were prepared and discussed with potential volunteers. For samples see items 12 through 16 on pages 68-72.

When the volunteer began her assignment, the Volunteer Record (Item 17, page 73) was completed by the parent coordinator. This form indicated the volunteer's supervisor, the days and times of volunteer service, and the record of the days the volunteer was absent. This information was maintained in the volunteer's file.

The parent coordinator prepared a volunteer schedule. The names of the volunteer supervisors were placed vertically on the left side of the chart and the days of the week were listed horizontally. A card containing the volunteer's name, address, phone number, and hours of the day worked was placed in the appropriate position. This chart gave a visual presentation of each parent's volunteer service.

Supervisors were asked to notify the parent coordinator when a volunteer was absent, and this fact was placed on that volunteer's record. Repeated absences resulted in a phone call to the parent by the coordinator inquiring if anyone could be of assistance. She also asked if the volunteer wished to continue in the program. The most frequent reasons given for absence were illness and doctor's appointments.

Some volunteers indicated a preference to work only on special programs and activities instead of committing themselves to a specific time each week. A Volunteer Record—Special Programs and Activities (Item 18, page 74) was maintained for these volunteers. This form includes a record of the activities in which the volunteer participated and provides a list of experienced volunteers for future reference.

Orienting and Training Parent Volunteers

Orientation acquaints the volunteer with the school district and with the procedures and goals of the parent volunteer program. Training, on the other hand, is designed to impart skills and techniques needed in a specific job or assignment. The orientation should be given at the school site before the volunteer begins work, thus providing the opportunity to become acquainted with the personnel and facilities. The orientation should be designed to increase the parent's self-confidence. It is important that the staff contact provide a warm and welcome reception to the volunteer, giving a sense of belonging.

Orientation and training may take place in formal meetings, informal discussion groups, coffee klatches, or any combination of these.

It is helpful to include coverage of the following subjects in parent volunteer orientation programs:

1. Importance of the volunteer program.
2. General philosophy of the district and school and overview of the entire program.
3. Goals and objectives of the parent volunteer program, school, and district.
4. Introduction to the staff, school plant, and pertinent policies and procedures.
5. Professional ethics, including appropriate dress and confidentiality.
6. Communications with students, staff, community, and other volunteers.
7. The importance of working together cooperatively.
8. Health clearance.
9. Responsibilities of the school volunteer.

IMPLEMENTATION PHASE

Training techniques may include lectures, role playing, workshops, buzz or "rap" sessions, use of video or audio tapes, panel discussions, recordings, films, demonstrations by specialists, question and answer periods, brainstorming, field trips, and observation. These training techniques may be used separately or in any combination by parents or staff members who are knowledgeable about parent volunteer programs. The length of the training will depend upon the techniques and the individual responsible for the training, as well as the qualifications of those being trained. Sometimes colleges or high school credit may be arranged through local schools for parent volunteers during the training.

Listed below are some of the areas related to instruction that should be included in the training of classroom or media center volunteers.

1. Basic knowledge of teaching techniques.
2. How children learn, principles of human growth and development, and general characteristics of the group or individuals the volunteer will be assisting.
3. Individual tutoring.
4. Resources, materials, and equipment available for use.
5. The physical arrangement of the classroom.
6. Information regarding assisting with classroom control.
7. Reading of pertinent books and periodicals.

Some good materials are available to assist with parent volunteer training. Some districts have already produced publications which may prove helpful in a variety of subjects. *Parents and Teachers Together for the Benefit of Children* is the title of a multimedia action program produced by National Education Association Publications. This kit includes a two-part filmstrip, overhead transparencies, a booklet, and a comprehensive teacher guide that covers all aspects of planning and implementing a parent volunteer program. Also included are leaflets for distribution, posters, a cassette tape, name tags, and a workshop plan. This program can be obtained from the National Education Association, Publication-Sales Section 26, 1201 Sixteenth Street N.W., Washington, D.C. 20036.

In the model program, orientation for the volunteers began immediately after the initial interview with the supervisor. Each parent was given a pamphlet entitled *Orientation for Parent Volunteers* (Item 19, page 75), which includes an introduction, the goals of the program, the educational organization, a description of the school site, information on volunteer assignments, a few hints on working with students, and other items of interest. Each staff member also received a copy of this pamphlet so that she would know what information had been given to the parent volunteers. The presentation made by the resource teacher at the parent tea also served as a means of orienting volunteers. Meetings were held periodically with parents, the parent coordinator, and resource teacher in attendance to orient and train parents. Other materials relating to parent volunteer programs were made available to both volunteers and supervisors in the school library-media center (Item 7, page 61). Parent volunteers were made aware of these publications in the *Orientation for Parent Volunteers* pamphlet.

Each supervisor was asked by the resource teacher to provide on-the-job training for the volunteers who worked with her. This method provided for relevant training to accomplish the specific tasks to which the volunteer was assigned.

Supervisors were encouraged by the resource teacher to allow parents to become oriented to the environment in which they would be working before they began on-the-job training. In all cases, the first step of the training for the volunteers working in the classroom was to learn the students' names. Parents were then trained by their supervisors to assist with work at art stations and interest centers, to help children form letters, to listen to them read aloud, and to tell stories. Each parent was provided with a Volunteer Self-Evaluation (Item 20, page 79) to encourage introspection and analysis of ways volunteer performance could be improved.

The training of the parents prepared them to cope with their duties as volunteers, but observation indicated that the attitudes displayed toward children were ultimate determinants of success or failure by the volunteers. Supervisors endeavored to instill in the parent volunteers awareness of the need for praise and reinforcement, the fact that every student must know some measure of success if he is to learn. Volunteers were trained by supervisors to provide ways of allowing students to succeed. After each lesson, volunteers were encouraged to ask themselves, "What success did this child have with the lesson?"

Recognizing Volunteer Service

Recognition of the volunteers' contributions is most important and may include (1) on-the-job praise, (2) a yearly banquet, (3) certificates of recognition, (4) letters of appreciation, (5) a newsletter developed and distributed by parents, (6) presentation of various types of awards or pins for services provided, and (7) recognition through the news media.

It is perhaps obvious, but still worth emphasizing, that day-to-day recognition of the volunteers' contribution is important. Common courtesy and expressions of appreciation on the part of a school staff will pay many dividends.

In the Washington School model, one way of recognizing the volunteer service was to express continuing verbal appreciation for jobs which were well done. All of the supervisors were encouraged by the resource teacher and parent coordinator to make this an active part of their relationship with the volunteers.

Also, each volunteer received a "Very Important Parent Award" (Item 21, page 81) with her name inscribed on it. The principal and resource teacher requested that each supervisor write a letter of appreciation to the volunteers who worked with her. Supervisors were also encouraged to ask students to write "thank you" letters. An article was submitted to the local paper listing the volunteers by name as well as some of the services they provided.

The recognition given volunteers by the Washington School staff was not the only factor that encouraged the parents to return and continue working with students. The parents who volunteered for a second year stated that they found their work personally rewarding.

In summary, both supervisors and volunteers indicate that some children need the assurance of helpful adults, and parents bring more of this dimension of caring to the students than it is possible for the assigned teacher alone to do. Parents have commented that, as the self-respect of the students increased, their need for assistance from the volunteer parents diminished.

At Washington School, each student was treated as an individual with expectations, abilities, and interests different from those of other students. Developing positive personal relationships with adults enhanced the student's education. In fact, the opportunity to develop positive adult-student relationships is beneficial both to children and to adutls.

The implementation of a parent volunteer program as described in this chapter can assist in achieving such benefits.

[ITEM 4.]

WASHINGTON SCHOOL
Selma, California 93662

ORIENTATION INFORMATION FOR PARENT VOLUNTEER SUPERVISORS

PURPOSES:

The purposes of this pamphlet are to provide members of the Washington Elementary School staff who will be supervising parent volunteers with information which will (1) delineate their responsibilities for orienting and training volunteers and (2) present some considerations when working with parent volunteers.

ORIENTING AND
TRAINING PARENTS:

The parent volunteers at Washington School will be oriented before they begin their responsibilities under your supervision. Selma Unified School District and Washington School policies, goals of the parent volunteer program, communications, professional ethics will be covered, and a tour of the school plant will be given. You will be asked to orient the volunteer regarding your own specific policies and procedures and provide on-the-job training for the duties you will assign. This instruction may be given at any time which is convenient for you and the volunteer. Be specific so the volunteer will know what you want done and how you want it accomplished.

Please familiarize the volunteer with your emergency procedures, including fire drills and civil defense procedures.

Keep your on-the-job training practical. Most parents will be more interested in accomplishments than in theories.

Please do not allow the volunteer to handle confidential material, including cumulative folders.

The training you provide should consider the parent's interests and abilities. Experience may indicate after a period of time that some of the duties you have assigned may need to be altered. If you feel a parent is not meeting with success in some of the responsibilities you assigned to her, then talk it over with the volunteer. You may agree it is feasible to shift her to other duties or to give additional training to assist the volunteer in coping with the present assignment.

[ITEM 4. Continued]

GETTING STARTED:

Prepare the pupils for an extra adult in the classroom by introducing her to the class and explaining her duties. She should be introduced to other staff members at Washington School, including the principal, custodian, aides, and teachers. The parent coordinator will have already met her. Time spent on these introductions will not be wasted because it will help provide the volunteer with a feeling of belonging.

The first few visits the volunteer makes to the school will be most important ones. It might be helpful to request all parent volunteers to observe students for a period of time before they actually start working with them. This will give you time to assess the parent's interests and abilities and provide her with some confidence. Most volunteers want to feel needed; thus meaningful tasks that do not require direct involvement with students should be assigned shortly after they arrive. These duties might include cutting paper or preparing a bulletin board. Volunteers should be made to feel useful as quickly as possible.

ESTABLISHING CONFIDENCE:

This will be the first experience most parents have had as a volunteer in an educational environment. Their confidence may be increased by (1) being greeted as a friend from the very beginning, (2) providing a thorough training program, (3) having duties assigned commensurate with their interests and abilities, and (4) being complimented.

You can also demonstrate your confidence in the parent by sharing some of the work that requires imagination and creativity with her. All of us want to feel our ideas are accepted and worthwhile; it may help you to ask for the parent's suggestions.

OTHER CONSIDERATIONS:

If you do not already have individual work stations, it might be helpful to set up one or two in an area of the room where a parent can work with students individually.

Be responsible for your own discipline and do not encourage the volunteer to discipline for you. Previous experience of some teachers suggests that when parents are in the room the discipline generally improves.

[ITEM 4. Continued]

It also may be helpful for you to arrange with the volunteer for periodic meetings to evaluate her progress and discuss any problems which may arise.

With the exception of the office assistants, the volunteers are to work under the direct supervision of a credentialed staff member. In the classroom, volunteers should not (1) diagnose student needs, (2) prescribe instructional materials, (3) orient or teach content, and (4) evaluate student achievement.

The relationship you have with the volunteer is important. If you feel conflicts beginning, talk them over with the parent. If this does not resolve the situation, then discuss the conflicts with the parent coordinator or the principal. If a satisfactory solution cannot be reached, the parent may be reassigned or asked to contribute in some other manner.

LIBRARY MATERIALS:

A small reference library for supervisors and volunteers is available in the media center. If you feel additional information regarding parent volunteer programs or orienting-training volunteers may be helpful, consult the library to determine if a publication is available which may meet your needs.

[ITEM 5]

WASHINGTON SCHOOL
Selma, California 93662

VOLUNTEER ATTENDANCE RECORD

Supervisor _____ Room Number _____

INSTRUCTIONS: Please maintain a running total of the hours each volunteer you supervise contributes.

Month
October
Volunteer:
_____ 1 2 3 4 5 6 7 8 9 10 11 12 13 14 15 16 17 18 19 20 21 22 23 24
_____ 1 2 3 4 5 6 7 8 9 10 11 12 13 14 15 16 17 18 19 20 21 22 23 24
_____ 1 2 3 4 5 6 7 8 9 10 11 12 13 14 15 16 17 18 19)0 21 22 23 24

November
Volunteer:
_____ 1 2 3 4 5 6 7 8 9 10 11 12 13 14 15 16 17 18 19 20 21 22 23 24
_____ 1 2 3 4 5 6 7 8 9 10 11 12 13 14 15 16 17 18 19 20 21 22 23 24
_____ 1 2 3 4 5 6 7 8 9 10 11 12 13 14 15 16 17 18 19 20 21 22 23 24

December
Volunteer:
_____ 1 2 3 4 5 6 7 8 9 10 11 12 13 14 15 16 17 18 19 20 21 22 23 24
_____ 1 2 3 4 5 6 7 8 9 10 11 12 13 14 15 16 17 18 19 20 21 22 23 24
_____ 1 2 3 4 5 6 7 8 9 10 11 12 13 14 15 16 17 18 19 20 21 22 23 24

January
Volunteer:
_____ 1 2 3 4 5 6 7 8 9 10 11 12 13 14 15 16 17 18 19 20 21 22 23 24
_____ 1 2 3 4 5 6 7 8 9 10 11 12 13 14 15 16 17 18 19 20 21 22 23 24
_____ 1 2 3 4 5 6 7 8 9 10 11 12 13 14 15 16 17 18 19 20 21 22 23 24

February
Volunteer:
_____ 1 2 3 4 5 6 7 8 9 10 11 12 13 14 15 16 17 18 19 20 21 22 23 24
_____ 1 2 3 4 5 6 7 8 9 10 11 12 13 14 15 16 17 18 19 20 21 22 23 24
_____ 1 2 3 4 5 6 7 8 9 10 11 12 13 14 15 16 17 18 19 20 21 22 23 24

March
Volunteer:
_____ 1 2 3 4 5 6 7 8 9 10 11 12 13 14 15 16 17 18 19 20 21 22 23 24
_____ 1 2 3 4 5 6 7 8 9 10 11 12 13 14 15 16 17 18 19 20 21 22 23 24
_____ 1 2 3 4 5 6 7 8 9 10 11 12 13 14 15 16 17 18 19 20 21 22 23 24

[ITEM 6]

WASHINGTON SCHOOL
Selma, California 93662

VOLUNTEER INFORMATION

Instructions: Please return to the resource teacher one of these forms for each volunteer. Not all questions will be applicable to all volunteers. If the question does not apply, please place a check ( ) on the line next to the letters NA.

_____ _____ _____
   Supervisor's Name   Room Number   Parent's Name

1. How many students do you have in your class?_____

2. How many hours each month did this parent assist you? (Fill in the number of hours.)
Sept._____ Oct._____ Nov._____ Dec._____ Jan._____
Feb._____ Mar._____ Apr._____ May_____ June_____

3. Please list what this volunteer accomplished under your supervision and the approximate percentage of her volunteer time spent at the task.

4. How many students in your class have received two or more hours of individual instruction from this parent volunteer?_____ NA_____. (Individual instruction is defined for this purpose as being instruction of any type given to a student by a volunteer on a one-to-one basis.)

5. How many students received enrichment lessons or activities from this volunteer?_____NA_____(Enrichment lessons or activities are defined here as experiences provided by volunteers which broaden student understanding of teacher introduced topics.)

6. How many non-English speaking students do you have? _____ NA_____.
Does this parent speak Spanish? Yes_____ No_____.
How many non-English speaking students, if any, did this parent instruct over two hours? _____ NA_____.

[ITEM 7]

WASHINGTON SCHOOL
Selma, California 93662

LIBRARY PUBLICATIONS

The following sources of information are available in the library. You may use the material there or check it out. Each of these publications has been carefully selected for pertinent content.

Chambers, Jewell C., ed. *ABC's. . . . A Handbook for Educational Volunteers.* Washington, D.C.: Washington Technical Institute, 1972.

Educational Service Bureau, Inc. *School Volunteers.* Washington, D.C. Educational Service Bureau, Inc., 1966.

Ferver, Jack, and Doris M. Cook. *Teacher Aides—Handbook for Instructors and Administrators.* Madison: The University of Wisconsin, 1970.

Fresno County Department of Education. *Educational Aide—Member of the School Team.* Fresno, California: 1970.

Harrison, Raymond H. *The Selection, Orientation, and Use of Teacher Aides.* Fresno, California: G. W. School Supply, 1971.

Hornburger, Jane M. *So You Have an Aide.* Wilmington, Delaware: Wilmington Public Schools, 1970.

Hubley, John W. *School Volunteer Programs . . . How They Are Organized and Managed.* Worthington, Ohio: School Management Institute, Inc., 1972.

National Education Association. *Teacher Aides at Work.* Washington, D. C.: National Education Association, 1967.

San Diego City Schools. *A Handbook for Teacher Assistants and Teacher Aides: Primary Grades.* San Diego, California: 1968.

San Diego City Schools. *A Handbook for Parent Volunteer Activities for Kindergarten and Primary Classrooms.* San Diego, California: 1969.

San Diego City Schools. *Your Aide and You: The Role of the Instructional Aide in the Elementary School.* San Diego, California: 1971.

Sayler, Mary Lou. *Parents: Active Partners in Education.* Washington, D. C.: American Association of Elementary-Kindergarten-Nursery Educators, 1971.

Schindler-Rainman, Eva, and Lois Williams. *Teaching and Reaching Children.* Montebello, California: Montebello Unified School District, 1970.

U. S. Department of Health, Education and Welfare, Office of Education, Bureau of Educational Personnel Development. *A Coordinator's "How to Do" Handbook.* Bethesda, Maryland: ERIC Document Reproduction Service, ED 067 731, 1971.

[ITEM 7. Continued]

U. S. Department of Health, Education and Welfare, Office of Child Development. *Project Head Start: Parent Involvement.* Washington, D. C.: Project Head Start.

U. S. Department of Health, Education and Welfare, Office of Education. *Meeting Parents Halfway.* Washington, D. C.: Government Printing Office, 1972.

U. S. Department of Health, Education and Welfare, Office of Education. *Parent Involvement in Title I E.S.E.A.—Why? What? How?* Washington, D.C.: Government Printing Office, 1972.

[ITEM 8]

WASHINGTON SCHOOL
Selma, California 93662

PARENT COORDINATOR JOB DESCRIPTION

I. The parent coordinator will work under the direct supervision of the principal.

II. Weekly time spent at the position will vary, but it is anticipated the average will be eight hours per week.

III. Duties will include:
    A. Assisting with public relations.
    B. Recruiting volunteers through personal contacts.
    C. Screening potential volunteers.
    D. Assisting with assigning and orienting parents.
    E. Assisting with routine operations including record keeping and contacting absent parents.
    F. Evaluating the program.
    G. Recognizing parent volunteer service.

IV. Materials and equipment will be provided, including a desk in the school office, telephone, and file cabinet.

[ITEM 9. INFORMATION LEAFLET—ENGLISH]

YOU CAN MAKE A DIFFERENCE . . . . .
                IN THE LIVES OF CHILDREN

A parent volunteer program is starting at Washington School and you are invited to participate. The program is designed to provide parents of Washington students with the opportunity to make a *real* contribution to the education of their children.

***   WHO QUALIFIES?
    . . . Any parent of a Washington student who is dependable, warm, thoughtful, and concerned.

***   HOW CAN YOU HELP?
    . . . Everyone has talents and you can share your concern with students by working in a classroom, assisting with supervision, working in the office or library and in many other ways.

***   WHEN DOES THE PROGRAM START?
    . . . As soon as you feel you want to help.

***   HOW DO YOU GET MORE INFORMATION?
    . . . Call Washington School—896-3415
    Mrs. Enedina Grijalva is the parent coordinator
    Mr. Jack Pell is the principal.

[ITEM 10. INFORMATION LEAFLET—SPANISH]

USTED PUEDE INLUER....

LAS VIDAS DE NINOS

Un programa de padres voluntarios se esta empezando en la escuela de Washington y se le invita a usted a participar. El proposito del programa es darles a los padres de los alumnos la oportunidad de contribuir a la educacion de sus hijos.

*** ?QUIEN TIENE LAS CALIFICACIONES?
...Cualquier madre o padre de un alumno de Washington que sea responsable, amable, atento y preoccupado.

*** ?COMO PUEDE AYUDAR USTED?
... Todo el mundo tiene talentos y usted puede usar los suyos a ayudar a los alumnos al trabajar en una clase, ayudar con la supervision, trabajar en la oficina o la biblioteca y en otras formas.

*** ?CUANDO EMPIEZA EL PROGRAMA?
... Tan pronto como usted este dispuesto a ayudar.

*** ?COMO PUEDE CONSEQUIR MAS INFORMACION?
... Llame a la escuela de Washington—896-3415 La Sra. Enedina Grijalva es la coordinadora de los padres. El Sr. Jack Pell es el director de la escuola.

[ITEM 11]

WASHINGTON SCHOOL
Selma, California 93662

VOLUNTEER QUESTIONNAIRE

Name _____ Date _____
        First   Middle   Last

Home Address _____ Phone _____

Business Address _____ Phone _____

Washington Elementary School Children:

Name	Teacher
Name	Teacher
Name	Teacher
Name	Teacher

(Please check the appropriate spaces)

Is transportation available to you? yes _____ no _____

Do you have a communicable disease or emotional disturbance? yes _____ no _____

If the answer is "yes," please explain here.

Do you have any physical limitations? yes _____ no _____
If the answer is "yes," please explain here.

Who is to be notified in case of an emergency?

Name _____

_____ Phone _____
        Address

[ITEM 11. Continued]

What type of past work experience have you had?

Do you speak Spanish? yes _____ no _____
Do you write Spanish? yes _____ no _____
How would you like to assist?
Clerical:
    _____ type   _____ run off dittos
    _____ interpret   _____ do general office work
    _____ make home calls   _____ make attendance phone calls

Supervision:
    _____ bus   _____ playground   _____ lunch

Classroom:
    _____ keep records (attendance)
    _____ make instructional materials
    _____ do small group tutoring
    _____ do individual tutoring

Health:
    _____ assist with vision/hearing screening
    _____ assist with health education

Library:
    _____ assist librarian

Special:
    _____ accompany students on field trips
    _____ other types of assistance (please explain)

When can you help? (The exact time of service will be by mutual agreement between the staff member and the volunteer.)

MONDAY   A.M _____ P.M. _____ After School _____
TUESDAY   A.M. _____ P.M. _____ After School _____
WEDNESDAY   A.M. _____ P.M. _____ After School _____
THURSDAY   A.M. _____ P.M. _____ After School _____
FRIDAY   A.M. _____ P.M. _____ After School _____
Any School Day   A.M. _____ P.M. _____ After School _____

Do you need a babysitter? yes _____ no _____
Why do you want to volunteer at Washington School?

[ITEM 12]

WASHINGTON SCHOOL
Selma, California 93662

LIBRARY ASSISTANT JOB DESCRIPTION

I. The library volunteer works under the direct supervision of the library aide in the library at Washington School.

II. Specific time arrangements will be made by mutual agreement between the parent volunteer and the library aide.

III. Library volunteer duties will include:

    A. Supervising learning game time.
    B. Filing cards.
    C. Arranging books on shelves.
    D. Reading stories to students.
    E. Helping students select books.
    F. Helping to color code, stamp, and glue pockets on books.

[ITEM 13]

WASHINGTON SCHOOL
Selma, California 93662

SECRETARIAL ASSISTANT JOB DESCRIPTION

I. The secretarial assistant will work under the direct supervision of the school secretary in the office at Washington School.

II. Specific time arrangements will be made by mutual agreement between the parent volunteer and the secretary.

III. Secretarial assistant duties will include:
- A. Receiving faculty, students, and guests at the office counter.
- B. Answering the telephone.
- C. Typing originals and dittos.
- D. Operating reproduction equipment.

[ITEM 14]

WASHINGTON SCHOOL
Selma, California 93662

ATTENDANCE CLERK JOB DESCRIPTION

I. The attendance clerk will work under the direct supervision of the principal and school secretary in the office and community surrounding Washington School.

II. Specific time arrangements will be made by mutual agreement between the parent volunteer and the school secretary.

III. Attendance clerk duties will include:
    A. Interviewing students regarding attendance.
    B. Making telephone calls to students' homes.
    C. Making home calls.

[ITEM 15]

WASHINGTON SCHOOL
Selma, California 93662

GROUNDS SUPERVISOR JOB DESCRIPTION

I. The grounds supervisor will work under the direct supervision of the principal on the Washington School grounds.

II. Specific time arrangements will be made by mutual agreement between the parent volunteer and the principal.

III. Grounds supervisor duties will include:
   A. Issuing playground equipment.
   B. Assisting students with playground activities.
   C. Patrolling student rest rooms.
   D. Encouraging students to participate in activities.

If the volunteer is available before and/or after school, duties may include supervising bus loading and/or unloading.

[ITEM 16]

WASHINGTON SCHOOL
Selma, California 93662

HEALTH ASSISTANT JOB DESCRIPTION

I. The health assistant will work under the direct supervision of the school nurse in the nurse's office at Washington School.

II. Hours per week would vary depending on health needs and volunteer time. Specific time arrangements will be made by mutual agreement of the parent volunteer and school nurse.

III. Health service duties will include:
  A. Checking the list of students to be tested and calling students from class.
  B. Taking and recording height and weight.
  C. Giving students a cup to obtain urine and recording urinalysis.

[ITEM 17]

WASHINGTON SCHOOL
Selma, California 93662

VOLUNTEER RECORD

_____   _____   _____
Volunteer's Name   Supervisor   Date

The volunteer reports at the following times each week:

DAY	ARRIVES	DEPARTS
Monday	_____	_____
Tuesday	_____	_____
Wednesday	_____	_____
Thursday	_____	_____
Friday	_____	_____

The volunteer has been absent the following days:

	School Notified in Advance	
DATE	YES	NO
_____	_____	_____
_____	_____	_____
_____	_____	_____
_____	_____	_____
_____	_____	_____
_____	_____	_____
_____	_____	_____
_____	_____	_____
_____	_____	_____
_____	_____	_____

[ITEM 18]

WASHINGTON SCHOOL
Selma, California 93662

VOLUNTEER RECORD

Special Programs and Activities Volunteers

Volunteer's Name	Address	Phone Number

This parent has volunteered and participated in the following activities:

ACTIVITY	DATE

[ITEM 19]

WASHINGTON SCHOOL
Selma, California 93662

ORIENTATION FOR PARENT VOLUNTEERS

Welcome to Washington School

PURPOSE:

The purpose of this pamphlet is to provide information for you as a new volunteer at Washington School. Please read this carefully and feel free to ask the parent coordinator, Mrs. Grijalva, the principal, Mr. Pell, or the resource teacher, Mrs. Say, any questions.

INTRODUCTION:

The goals of the parent volunteer program at Washington School are to: (1) strengthen home/community-school relations, (2) provide individual instruction for Washington students, (3) provide enrichment activities, (4) provide instruction for non-English speaking students in their own language, and (5) increase children's motivation for learning.

There are many advantages of a parent volunteer program. One is that family-school relationships may be improved. Educational benefits for a child may also be improved with support from the home and with close liaison between the home and the school.

The motivation of students can also be increased. As students see their own parents involved in school affairs, they become encouraged to take a more active interest themselves in education.

Each child is important and should receive individual instruction, but when there are many students in a class it is difficult for a teacher to provide the attention that each child needs. Your assistance in the classroom, on the playground, in the office, or working with the nurse can help provide the individual attention most pupils require. In fact, a requirement of the Early Childhood Education program is that students be given individualized instruction.

School and community relationships may also be improved. You can be an ambassador of good will for Selma's schools. Your visible sign of support through volunteering time is a demonstration to others that you are concerned.

[ITEM 19. Continued]

ORGANIZATION:

The line of responsibility in the educational system is diagrammed below:

State Department of Education
Dr. Wilson Riles

Fresno County Department of Education
Mr. Ernest Poore

Selma Unified School District
Dr. Bob Blancett

Elementary Instruction
Mr. Bill Heavner

Washington Elementary School
Mr. Jack Pell

Parent	Resource
Coordinator	Teacher
Mrs. Enedina Grijalva	Mrs. Gwen Say

You may obtain information, advice, or guidance from your supervisor, resource teacher, parent coordinator, or the principal.

SCHOOL SITE:

You will be given a tour of Washington School to acquaint you with the facilities, including the location of lavatories, work room, and offices. Your supervisor will provide a detailed explanation of the physical area in which you will be working.

ASSIGNMENT:

Every effort will be made to assign you to duties related to your interests and abilities consistent with the needs of the staff. If you are not satisfied with your assignment, please contact Mrs. Grijalva, Mrs. Say, or Mr. Pell, and other arrangements will be made. Sometimes the needs of the teacher and the class also change; thus under some circumstances assignments may be shifted by Mr. Pell or Mrs. Say.

[ITEM 19. Continued]

WORKING WITH STUDENTS:

The following guidelines may be helpful to you while working with students. More specific instructions will be given to you by your supervisor.

    1. Learn the names of pupils quickly and use them frequently. Most teachers have a seating chart which will be helpful to you.

    2. Learn as much as possible about the pupils and show an interest in them.

    3. Give encouragement to pupils whenever and wherever possible. Compliment them for work well done and praise them for effort.

    4. Be attentive to children when they speak. Do not be afraid to demonstrate that you enjoy working with them.

    5. Be consistent in your behavior and attitude toward children. They deserve the security that comes from knowing where adults who work with them stand.

OTHER CONSIDERATIONS:

The teacher is responsible for the learning program and classroom climate. You are asked not to discuss a teacher's techniques or actions with parents, other instructors, or children. Please remember you are under the direct supervision of a credentialed instructor. If you have a question regarding what is taking place in the classroom, speak to the teacher or the principal. Problems and information concerning pupils or members of the staff are considered *confidential*. Please do not discuss any school business with anyone except your supervisor, the parent coordinator, the resource teacher, or the principal.

    Volunteers should not discipline children. You may be firm, but it is the responsibility of the teacher to discipline each child. You may wish to bring a student's actions to the attention of your supervisor so that she may take corrective measures.

    Your role at Washington School is a complementary one to the existing staff. Your abilities and talents are needed, but the staff's directions must be followed at all times. They are responsible for the education that takes place in the classrooms. If you feel a misunderstanding is taking place, talk it over with your supervisor immediately. This can save many hard feelings.

[ITEM 19. Continued]

Any accident you observe involving either children, volunteers, or paid staff should be reported to the office immediately. You are covered by insurance while working at Washington School.

Political activity at the school site is prohibited by district policy and state law. The distribution of any materials without the principal's permission is forbidden.

Other people are depending on you so please make every effort to be punctual and attend regularly. If for some reason you will be late or unable to report, please notify the office at 896-3415 so other arrangements can be made.

LIBRARY MATERIAL:

A small library for supervisors and volunteers is available in the media center. If you wish to do further reading about parent volunteer programs consult the media center to determine if a publication is there which might interest you.

[ITEM 20]

WASHINGTON SCHOOL
Selma, California 93662

VOLUNTEER SELF-EVALUATION

INSTRUCTIONS: Please check one of the three boxes opposite each question.

	Yes	Sometimes	No
1. Do I plan for the activity to which I have been assigned?			
2. Do I make myself helpful by offering my services to the teacher when there is an obvious need for help?			
3. Do I observe closely so that I can become acquainted with the children's likes, dislikes, preferences, enthusiasms, and aversions?			
4. Do I find opportunities for giving students choices or do I tell them what to do?			
5. Do I emphasize the times when students do well and minimize the times when they fail?			
6. Do I really listen to what students have to say?			
7. Do I accept criticisms and suggestions objectively?			
8. Do I follow directions of the supervisor?			
9. Do I try to develop a friendly attitude with all of my co-workers?			
10. Do I give the supervisor adequate notice of absences?			
11. Do I realize that my whole purpose for being in the classroom is to assist the teacher in order that the students might progress more rapidly?			

[ITEM 20. Continued]

12. Do I refrain from interfering between a teacher and student unless called upon for assistance?
13. Do I avoid criticism of the student, teacher, and the school?
14. Do I have good rapport with the students?
15. Do I have good rapport with the teacher?

[ITEM 21]

VIP
Very Important Parent
AWARD

Presented to

_____

In Honor and with deep appreciation of the faithful, devoted, and valuable service given to our school.

_____

Presented this _____ day of _____ 19 ___

CHAPTER IV

Evaluation Phase

Introduction

Evaluation is the means of determining the degree of success with which a program meets the preestablished goals and objectives. Without cearly stated goals and objectives, it is almost impossible to evaluate program efforts. Interviews, questionnaires, observations, logs and records, as well as anecdotal observations, various types of reports, and case studies may be used in the evaluation process. Outside agencies, consultants, or specialists may be engaged, but more frequently, evaluation is performed by those people actually participating in the program. The instruments needed for in-house

EVALUATION PHASE

evaluations are included in this chapter's exhibits, items 22 through 26, pages 87-92.

It is important that parents and staff members participating in the program be aware of the evaluation criteria used throughout the implementation phase. The data gathered for each objective should be easily tabulated and lend themselves to easy display.

Evaluating Objectives

At Washington School, the evaluation instrument entitled Observed Results (Item 22, page 87), provides opportunity for volunteers and staff members to rate each component of the program and the degree to which the volunteer program strengthens home/community-school relations and increases children's motivation to learn. To determine motivation, it provides the information needed regarding the student responses to the faces on the handout.

The returned Volunteer Information sheets (chapter III, Item 6, page 60) provide the data necessary to determine if the objectives relating to individual instruction, enrichment lessons, and bilingual instruction for non-English-speaking students were being met.

The cover letter (Item 23, page 89) provides the information needed by teachers to gather the data from the student handout (Item 24, page 90).

The following review will relate the instruments to the objectives:

Objective: When staff members and parents are asked the question "Did the program strengthen home/community-school relations?" a minimum mean value of four on a scale of seven will be obtained.

The total numerical score assigned to question one on the instrument entitled Observed Results divided by the number of instruments returned will provide the mean value assigned by the evaluators.

Objective: During the school year fifty parents will participate in the parent volunteer program.

One Volunteer Information sheet was returned by parent volunteer supervisors for each volunteer. These were counted and the resulting figure was the number of parents assisting in the program.

Objective: Twenty-five percent of the students will receive two or more hours of individual instruction from a parent volunteer.

The Volunteer Information sheet contains the question "How many students in your class have received two or more hours of individual instruction from this parent volunteer?" The percentage of the students receiving individual instruction can be determined by dividing the number of students in the school into the total number of students receiving the instruction.

Objective: Twenty-five percent of the students will receive an enrichment lesson or activity presented by a parent.

Question one on the Volunteer Information sheets was tabulated and yielded the number of students to divide into the number which received enrichment lessons (question five on the Volunteer Information sheet). The resulting figure was the percentage receiving an enrichment lesson.

Objective: Fifty percent of the non-English-speaking students will receive two or more hours of individual instruction in English from a Spanish speaking volunteer.

The responses to question six on the Volunteer Information sheet yielded the necessary data to determine if this objective was met. The number of non-

English-speaking students divided into the number of students receiving instruction by a Spanish speaking parent will provide the percentage figure.

Objective: When students are read the question "How do you feel about having someone else's parent help you here at school?" a greater number will respond by selecting the happy face than the neutral or unhappy faces on a handout provided by the teacher.

When the Observed Results forms are returned, the responses to question number nine may be added to determine if this objective was met.

Objective: When staff members and parents are asked the question "Did the use of parent volunteers increase the children's motivation for learning?" a minimum mean value of four on a scale of seven will be obtained.

The total numerical scores tabulated from question two on the instrument entitled Observed Results divided by the number of returned instruments will provide the mean value.

Objective: When staff members and parents are asked to rate each component of the parent volunteer program a minimum mean assigned value of four on a scale of seven will be obtained.

The total number of points obtained by each component divided by the number of responses will provide the mean score for each component to determine if this objective has been met.

The Evaluation Interview (Item 25, page 91) may be used to provide parents the opportunity to assess the program verbally. It may be helpful to those evaluating the program to talk with parents and record the interview on this form.

The Supervisor Evaluation of the Volunteer (Item 26, page 92) may be combined with personal observation to determine the strengths and weaknesses of parents participating in the program.

Periodic evaluation conferences were held throughout the program involving the parent coordinator, principal, resource teacher, staff, parents, and author to provide a continuous process by which information was gathered to update or modify the volunteer program.

Conclusion

Evaluation results assist in identifying the strengths and weaknesses of a parent volunteer program. These data, combined with the experiences of staff members, are essential to the development of a program which will have improved results each succeeding year.

[ITEM 22]

WASHINGTON SCHOOL
Selma, California 93662

OBSERVED RESULTS

INSTRUCTIONS: Please rate the success of the parent volunteer program by checking one of the seven boxes opposite each question or program component. Additional comments regarding the program are encouraged. Please return this to the resource teacher at your earliest convenience. Thank you.

SUCCESSFUL - UNSUCCESSFUL

	7	6	5	4	3	2	1
QUESTIONS	☐	☐	☐	☐	☐	☐	☐

1. Did the program strengthen home/community-school relations?
   COMMENTS:

2. Did the use of parent volunteers increase the children's motivation for learning? ☐ ☐ ☐ ☐ ☐ ☐ ☐
   COMMENTS:

PROGRAM COMPONENTS ☐ ☐ ☐ ☐ ☐ ☐ ☐

3. Orienting the Staff
   (Staff Only)
   COMMENTS:

[ITEM 22. Continued]

SUCCESSFUL - UNSUCCESSFUL

    7   6   5   4   3   2   1

4. Obtaining a Parent Coordinator
   ☐ ☐ ☐ ☐ ☐ ☐ ☐
   COMMENTS:

5. Public Relations and Recruiting Volunteers
   ☐ ☐ ☐ ☐ ☐ ☐ ☐
   COMMENTS:

6. Screening and Placing Volunteers
   ☐ ☐ ☐ ☐ ☐ ☐ ☐
   COMMENTS:

7. Orienting and Training Volunteers
   ☐ ☐ ☐ ☐ ☐ ☐ ☐
   COMMENTS:

8. Recognizing Volunteer Service
   ☐ ☐ ☐ ☐ ☐ ☐ ☐
   COMMENTS:

9. TEACHERS ONLY: When asked the question "How do you feel about having parents help you here at school?" how many students selected:
   HAPPY FACE_____ NEUTRAL FACE_____ UNHAPPY FACE_____

[ITEM 23. COVER LETTER]

WASHINGTON SCHOOL
Selma, California 93662

PARENT VOLUNTEER PROGRAM

Dear Faculty Member:

    The purpose of the attached handouts is to determine if parent volunteers increase a child's motivation for learning.

    Please pass out a sheet to each student. Instruct the students to place an X below the face they would like to pick when you read the question. Then please read the following question: "How do you feel about having parents help you here at school?"

    Collect the sheets, tabulate the results, and enter the data on the evaluation instrument entitled Observed Results.

    Thank you.

                          Sincerely,

                           Gwen Say
                           Resource Teacher

[ITEM 24]

WASHINGTON SCHOOL
Selma, California 93662

STUDENT HANDOUT

Room Number_____

[ITEM 25]

WASHINGTON SCHOOL
Selma, California 93662

EVALUATION INTERVIEW

_____   _____
Interviewee   Position

_____   _____ _____
Interviewer   Position   Date

1. What were the weaknesses of the program?

2. What suggestions do you have for improvement?

3. In your opinion, what were the highlights of the program?

4. What general comments or observations do you wish to make?

[ITEM 26]

WASHINGTON SCHOOL
Selma, California 93662

SUPERVISOR EVALUATION OF THE VOLUNTEER

_____   _____   _____   _____
Volunteer's name   # Hours of   Supervisor's Name   Date
                      Service

Please briefly describe the duties you assigned to the volunteer.

INSTRUCTIONS: Please rate the volunteer under your supervision by checking one of the five boxes opposite each item. Please return this to the parent coordinator at your earliest convenience.

Excellent ☐   Fair ☐   Unsatisfactory ☐
Good   ☐   Poor ☐

1. Demonstrates enthusiasm
2. Attends regularly
3. Establishes rapport with students
4. Establishes rapport with supervisor
5. Exercises good judgment
6. Follows through on given tasks
7. Follows directions
8. Is respectful and courteous
9. Shows initiative
10. Is accepted by students
11. Accepts responsibility
12. Is punctual
13. Displays a sense of humor
14. Uses tact
15. Performance with individual students
16. Performance with small groups
17. Appearance is appropriate

Should this volunteer be encouraged to continue in the program? Yes_____ No_____

Notes

Notes To Chapter I

[1]"Parent-Community Involvement in Early Childhood Education," *The Education Digest* (December, 1972): 45

[2]Earl S. Shoefer, "Toward a Revolution in Education: A Perspective from Child Development Research," *The National Elementary Principal* (September, 1971): 10.

[3]Interview with Wilson Riles, Superintendent of Public Instruction, State of California, Fresno, California, 17 October 1973.

[4]Benjamin S. Bloom, *Stability and Change in Human Characteristics* (Palo Alto, California: Scott, Foresman and Company, 1961), p. 205.

[5]James Milton Moler, "A Study of Good Parent Patricipation in Elementary Schools," Ed.D. dissertation, University of Virginia, 1958, quoted in University Microfilms Inc. *Dissertation Abstracts*, Volume XIX, Number 4, Ann Arbor, Michigan, October, 1958.

[6]Elizabeth McIntyre Ryan, "A Comparative Study of the Reading Achievement of Second Grade Pupils in Programs Characterized by a Contrasting Degree of Parent Participation," Ed.D. dissertation, Indiana University, 1964, quoted in University Microfilms Inc. *Dissertation Abstracts*, Volume XXV, Number 9, Ann Arbor, Michigan, March, 1965.

[7]Herbert Jerome Schiff, "The Effect of Personal Contactual Relationships on Parents' Attitudes Toward and Participation in Local School Affairs," Ed.D dissertation, Northwestern University, 1963, quoted in University Microfilms Inc. *Dissertation Abstracts*, Volume XXV, Number 1, Ann Arbor, Michigan, July, 1964.

[8]U.S. Department of Health, Education and Welfare, Office of Education, *Parent Involvement in Title I E.S.E.A.—Why? What? How?* (Washington, D.C.: Government Printing Office, 1972), p.3.

[9]Ibid., p. 4.

[10]Ibid., p. 3.

[11]U. S. Department of Health, Education and Welfare, Office of Child Development, *Project Head Start: Parent Involvement* (Washington, D.C.: Government Printing Office, 1969), p. 4.

Notes to Chapter III

[12]Gayle Janowitz, *Helping Hands: Volunteer Work in Education* (Chicago, Illinois: The University of Chicago Press, 1965), p. ix.

[13]U. S. Department of Health, Education and Welfare, Office of Education, Bureau of Educational Personnel Development, *A Coordinator's "How To Do" Handbook* (Bethesda, Maryland: ERIC Document Reproduction Service, ED 067 713, 1971), p. 67.

[14]"Parents Asked to Volunteer," *The Selma Enterprise*, 13 December 1973, p. 5.

APPENDIX A

Volunteer Organizations

The following listed school volunteer organizations are national in scope. Many state and local organizations have also been established.

The National School Volunteer Program was begun in 1964 with a grant from the Ford Foundation, 20 West 40th Street, New York, New York 10018.

The Association of Voluntary Action Scholars (AVAS) has been formed to generate the development and application of interdisciplinary research in the field of voluntary action. Incorporated as an independent, non-profit organization, AVAS is affiliated with the Center for a Voluntary Society, 1507 M Street N.W., Washington, D. C. 20005.

The Volunteer in Education (VIE) program is operated under the U. S. Office of Education. This program awards grants to assist local programs and develop state plans. The address is U. S. Office of Education, ROB 3, Room 4614, Seventh and D Streets S. W., Washington, D. C. 20202.

Other associations and agencies include Association of Voluntary Bureaus of America, P. O. Box 7253, Kansas City, Missouri 64113; National Center for Voluntary Action, 1735 I Street N. W., Washington, D. C. 20006; National Commission on Resources for Youth, 36 W. 44th Street, New York, New York 10035; and the National Reading Council, 1776 Massachusetts Avenue N. W., Washington, D. C. 20036.

APPENDIX B

Successful Programs

Many successful parent volunteer programs are in existence throughout the United States. The following are a few schools and school districts which have implemented parent volunteer programs. Self-evaluations indicate each of these programs has been successful.

    Bellefaire School, Cleveland, Ohio.
    Boise School District, Idaho.
    Denver Public Schools, Colorado.
    Los Angeles School District, California.
    Mamaroneck School, New York Public Schools.
    Mary M. Hooker School, Hartford, Connecticut.
    Modesto School District, California.
    Newark School District, New Jersey.

New York City Schools, New York.
Oakland City Schools, California.
Oakton Elementary School, Evanston, Illinois.
San Diego Unified School District, California.
San Francisco City Schools, California.
Tracy School, Norwalk, Connecticut.

Sources Consulted

I. Books, Pamphlets, and Government Publications

Association of California School Administrators. *Developing Programs in Early Childhood Education.* Burlingame, California: Association of California School Administrators, 1973.

Association of California School Administrators. *Handbook for Developing Programs in Early Childhood Education.* Burlingame, California: Association of California School Administrators, 1973.

Ayres, Leonard. *Laggards in Our Schools.* New York, New York, 1909, quoted in Janowitz, Gayle. *Helping Hands: Volunteer Work in Education.* Chicago, Illinois: The University of Chicago Press, 1965.

Bloom, Benjamin S. *Stability and Change in Human Characteristics.* Palo Alto, California: Scott, Foresman and Company, 1961.

California State Department of Education. *Education Code—1971.* Sacramento, California: 1971.

California State Department of Education. *Education for the People.* Sacramento, California: 1972.

California State Department of Education. *Education for the People, Volume I.* Sacramento, California: 1972.

California State Department of Education. *Education for the People, Volume II.* Sacramento, California: 1972.

California State Department of Education. *Goal: Goals and Objectives for Authentic Learning.* Sacramento, California: April 30, 1973.

California State Department of Education. *Policies for Early Childhood Education.* Sacramento, California: 1973.

California State Department of Education. *The Report of the Task Force on Early Childhood Education.* Sacramento, California: 1972.

Chambers, Jewell C., ed. *ABC's. . . . A Handbook for Educational Volunteers.* Washington, D. C.: Washington Technical Institute, 1972.

Educational Service Bureau, Inc. *School Volunteers.* Washington, D. C.: Educational Service Bureau, Inc., 1966.

Fever, Jack, and Cook, Davis M. *Teacher Aides—Handbook for Instructors and Administrators.* Madison, Wisconsin: The University of Wisconsin, 1970.

Fresno County Department of Education. *Educational Aide—Member of the School Team.* Fresno, California: 1970.

G. and C. Merriam Co. *Webster's New Collegiate Dictionary.* Springfield, Massachusetts: G. and C. Merriam Co., 1959.

Goodlad, John K. *Planning and Organizing for Teaching.* Project on the Instructional Program of Public Schools. Washington, D. C.: National Education Association, 1963.

Harrison, Raymond H. *The Selection, Orientation, and Use of Teacher Aides.* Fresno, California: G. W. School Supply, 1971.

Hill, Donna. *The Picture File: A Manual and Curriculum-Related Subject Heading List.* Hamden, Connecticut: Lin-

SOURCES CONSULTED

net Books, 1975. (Paper edition, Syracuse, New York: Gaylord Professional Publications, 1975.

Hornburger, Jane M. *So You Have an Aide*. Wilmington, Delaware: Wilmington Public Schools, 1970.

Hubley, John W. *School Volunteer Programs. . . . How They Are Organized and Managed*. Worthington, Ohio: School Management Institute, Inc., 1972.

Hymes, James L. *A Child Development Point of View*. Englewood Cliffs, New Jersey: Prentice-Hall, Inc., 1961.

Janowitz, Gayle. *Helping Hands: Volunteer Work in Education*. Chicago, Illinois: The University of Chicago Press, 1965.

Merced City Schools and Merced County Department of Education. *L.E.A.P. Project*. Merced, California: 1972.

Modesto City Schools. *Parent Involvement*. Modesto, California: 1973.

National Education Association. *Parent-Teacher Relationships*. Washington, D. C.: National Education Association, 1972.

National Education Association. *Teacher Aides at Work*. Washington, D. C.: National Education Association, 1967.

National School Public Relations Association. *School Volunteers: Districts Recruit Aides to Meet Rising Costs, Student Needs*. Arlington, Virginia: National School Public Relations Association, 1973.

National School Public Relations Association. *Working with Parents*. Washington, D. C.: National School Public Relations Association, 1968.

The New England Educational Assessment Project. *Teacher Aides in the Classroom*. New England Educational Assessment Project, 1968.

Oklahoma City Public Schools. *Guide for Volunteers in Mathematics*. Oklahoma City, Oklahoma: 1971.

Oklahoma City Public Schools. *Guide for the Volunteer in Sullivan and Distar Reading Programs*. Oklahoma City, Oklahoma: 1971.

Polette, Nancy. *The Vodka in the Punch and Other Notes from a Library Supervisor*. Hamden, Connecticut: Linnet Books, 1975.

Riverside Unified School District. *Harrison School Parent-Volunteer-Tutor Program: Working Through the Aide Maze.* Riverside, California: Riverside Unified School District, 1972.

San Diego City Schools. *A Handbook for Teacher Assistants and Teacher Aides: Primary Grades.* San Diego, California: 1968.

San Diego City Schools. *A Handbook for Parent Volunteer Activities for Kindergarten and Primary Classrooms.* San Diego, California: 1969.

San Diego City Schools. *Teacher Assistant Program.* San Diego, California: 1966.

San Diego City Schools. *The Role of the Paraprofessional in the Secondary School.* San Diego, California: 1967.

San Diego City Schools. *Your Aide and You: The Role of the Instructional Aide in the Elementary School.* San Diego, California: 1971.

Sayler, Mary Lou. *Individualized Instruction and the Grouping of Pupils.* Tustin, California: Individualized Instruction Association, 1968.

Sayler, Mary Lou. *Parents: Active Partners in Education.* Washington, D. C.: American Association of Elementary-Kindergarten-Nursery Educators, 1971.

Schindler-Rainmon, Eva, and Williams, Lois. *Teaching and Reaching Children.* Montebello, California: Montebello Unified School District, 1970.

Selma District Chamber of Commerce. *Community Economic Profile.* Selma, California: 1973.

Sleisenger, Lenore. *Guidebook for the Volunteer Reading Teacher.* New York: Teachers College Press, Columbia University, 1968.

Stout, Irving W., and Langdon, Grace. *What Research Says to the Teacher—Parent Teacher Relationships.* Washington, D. C.: National Education Association, 1958.

Texas Education Agency, Migrant and Preschool Programs. *A Teacher and Teacher Aide Guide for Programs for the Education of Migrant Children.* Austin, Texas: 1972.

Tulare County Child Care Educational Program. *Parent Involvement Manual.* Visalia, California: Tulare County Child Care Educational Program, 1973.

SOURCES CONSULTED

U. S. Department of Health, Education and Welfare, Office of Child Development. *Project Head Start, Parent Involvement.* Washington, D. C.: Project Head Start, 1972.

U. S. Department of Health, Education and Welfare, Office of Education. *Meeting Parents Halfway.* Washington, D. C.: Government Printing Office, 1972.

U. S. Department of Health, Education and Welfare, Office of Education. *Parent Involvement in Title I E.S.E.A.—Why? What? How?* Washington, D.C.: Government Printing Office, 1972.

Washington Technical Institute. *Project VOICE—Voluntary Opportunities for Inspiring Coordinators of Education.* Washington, D. C.: Washington Technical Institute, 1971.

Washington Technical Institute. *Volunteer Viewpoints.* Washington, D. C.: Washington Technical Institute, June, 1972.

Washington Technical Institute. *Volunteer Viewpoints.* Washington, D. C.: Washington Technical Institute, March, 1973.

II. Periodicals

Abbott, Jerry L. "Community Involvement: Everybody's Talking About It." *The National Elementary Principal* (January, 1973): 56-59.

Adamson, Gary. "Use of Volunteers in a School for Emotionally Disturbed Children." *Exceptional Children* (Summer, 1968): 757-758.

Criscuolo, Nicholas P. "Meaningful Parental Involvement in the Reading Program." *The National Elementary Principal* (April, 1972): 64-65.

Erb, Jane. "Springfield School Volunteers." *School and Community* (February, 1970): 14-15.

Fireside, Byrna J. "Use a Parent's Special Talent." *Instructor* (August/September, 1972): 57.

Frey, George T. "Improving School Community Relations." *Today's Education* (January, 1971): 14-17.

Goldring, Cynthia. "How to Cut Costs by Using Unpaid Volunteers." *The American School Board Journal* (May, 1972): 24-25.

Hickey, Howard W. "Recruiting, Training, Utilizing, and Evaluating Volunteers." *Community Education Journal* (July, 1973): 33-35.

Jordan, William C. "How to Put Parents to Work in the Classroom." *Nation's Schools* (February, 1968): 76-77.

Laing, Hugh B. "Using Parents Effectively in the School." *The Instructor* (February, 1972): 25.

Maerowitz, Inge. "Parents! Bless Them and Keep Them.... In Your Classroom." *The Education Digest* (March, 1973): 38-40.

Morgulos, Susan. "Teaching About Babe Ruth and Model T's." *Saturday Review of Education* (March, 1973): 66.

Moulton, Elizabeth. "School Volunteers: The National Scene." *Saturday Review of Education* (February, 1973): 39.

Norton, Michael N. "PR Program Runs Farther, Faster with Volunteer People Power!" *Thrust for Educational Leadership* (October, 1973): 22-23.

"Parent-Community Involvement in Early Childhood Education." *The Education Digest* (December, 1972): 45-47.

Parten, Carroll B. "A Training Program for Volunteers." *Young Children* (October, 1970): 27-33.

Rich, Leslie. "Newark's Parent-Powered School." *American Education* (December, 1971): 9-12.

Shoefer, Earl S. "Toward a Revolution in Education: A Perspective from Child Development Research." *National Elementary Principal* (September, 1971): 19.

Schoeller, Arthur W., and Pearson, David A. "Better Reading Through Volunteer Reading Tutors." *The Reading Teacher* (April, 1970): 625-630.

Shaw, Jack; Otte, Row W.; and Keister, Margaret M. "Helping Parents Understand the School Program." *The Instructor* (June/July, 1969): 16.

Shelby, Evelyn. "Tipping the Balance: The School Volunteer." *Saturday Review of Education* (February, 1973): 36-39.

Smith, Mildred B. "To Educate Children Effectively We Must Involve Parents." *The Instructor* (August/September, 1970): 119-121.

SOURCES CONSULTED

Taylor, Judith. "Involving Parents in Classroom Activities." *Instructor* (August/September, 1972): 54-58.

Thompson, Diane D., and Tobin, Michael F. "Unpaid Volunteers Pay Off for Inter-City Schools." *The National Elementary Principal* (October, 1971): 60-62.

"Use of Red Cross Volunteers in the School Health Program." *The Journal of School Health* (October, 1971): 428.

Van Willigen, John, and Spence, Allyn G. "Parents and Schools: Participation." *School and Community* (November, 1972): 21.

Wall, Kenneth. "Parents Can Be Private Tutors." *Instructor* (August/September, 1972): 54-55.

Willmon, Betty. "Parent Participation as a Factor in the Effectiveness of Head gstart Programs." *The Journal of Educational Research* (May/June, 1969): 406-410.

Zubkoff, Myrtle. "They Want to Help." *Instructor* (August/September, 1972): 54-55.

III. Microforms

Bookhart, Norma. *Handbook for Volunteer Reading Aides.* Bethesda, Maryland: ERIC Document Reproduction Service, ED 061 498, 1972.

Canadian Teachers Federation. *Paraprofessional School Personnel. Bibliographies in Education, No. 16.* Bethesda, Maryland: ERIC Document Reproduction Service, ED 048 102, 1970.

Community Services Planning Council. *The Neighborhood Study Center Teacher Aide Program.* Bethesda, Maryland: ERIC Document Reproduction Service, ED 060 164, 1970.

Fresno City Unified School District. *Using Volunteers in Compensatory Education.* Bethesda, Maryland: ERIC Document Reproduction Service, ED 001 461, 1965.

Gordon, Ira J. *Parent Involvement in Compensatory Education.* Bethesda, Maryland: ERIC Document Reproduction Service, ED 039 954, 1970.

Hawkins, Warren. *Volunteers in the School Health Program.*

Bethesda, Maryland: ERIC Document Reproduction Service, ED 031 442, 1967.

Janowitz, Gayle. *After School Study Centers: Experimental Materials and Clinical Research.* Bethesda, Maryland: ERIC Document Reproduction Service, ED 051 342, 1968.

Janowitz, Gayle. *After-School Study Centers: Volunteer Work in Reading.* Bethesda, Maryland: ERIC Document Reproduction Service, ED 001 751, 1964.

Lockhart, John. *Guide for Volunteers in Mathematics.* Bethesda, Maryland: ERIC Document Reproduction Service, ED 065 339, 1971.

Los Angeles City Schools. *How to Organize a School Volunteer Program in Individual Schools and Suggested Volunteer Aids.* Bethesda, Maryland: ERIC Document Reproduction Service, ED 036 463, 1968.

Montgomery Community Action Agency. *Information for the Volunteer Tutor.* Bethesda, Maryland: ERIC Document Reproduction Service, ED 049 417, 1971.

Program for Action by Citizens in Education. *Early Reading Assistance. A Reading Tutorial Program.* Bethesda, Maryland: ERIC Document Reproduction Service, ED 041 722, 1968.

Radin, Norma. *Three Degrees of Parent Involvement in a Pre-School Program: Impact on Mothers and Children.* Bethesda, Maryland: ERIC Document Reproduction Service, ED 052 831, 1971.

Runyon, Joyce M. *Administering Programs for Volunteer Services for the Gifted.* Bethesda, Maryland: ERIC Document Reproduction Service, ED 057 516, 1971.

Shalen, Marcia. *The School Volunteer Program.* Bethesda, Maryland: ERIC Document Reproduction Service, ED 010 743, 1966.

Staley, Gerald J. *Volunteer Aides in Public Schools. Policies and Procedures in Oregon and Washington.* Bethesda, Maryland: ERIC Document Reproduction Service, ED 041 862, 1970.

Stavos, Denny. *The Evaluation of the School Volunteer Project, 1970-1971.* Bethesda, Maryland: ERIC Document Reproduction Service, ED 059 331, 1971.

U. S. Department of Health, Education and Welfare, Office of Citizen Participation. *Volunteers in Education: Materials for Volunteer Programs and the Volunteer.* Bethesda, Maryland: ERIC Document Reproduction Service, ED 039 306, 1970.

U. S. Department of Health, Education and Welfare, Office of Education, Bureau of Educational Personnel Development. *A Coordinator's "How To Do" Handbook.* Bethesda, Maryland: ERIC Document Reproduction Service, ED 067 731, 1971.

U. S. Department of Health, Education and Welfare, Office of Education, Bureau of Research. *Paraprofessionals and Teacher Aides: An Annotated Bibliography.* Bethesda, Maryland: ERIC Document Reproduction Service, ED 036 492, 1970.

IV. Interviews

Berger, Betty. Vice-Principal, Gateway Elementary School, Silver Springs, Maryland. Personal interview, 19 July 1973.

Berne, Dale. Principal, Eastridge High School, Rochester, New York. Personal Interview, 20 July 1973.

Biggs, Kenneth L. Coordinator—Goals and Objectives, Fresno County Department of Education. Telephone interview, 28 September 1973.

Dominguez, Moses. Director of Special Projects, Selma Unified School District, Selma, California. Personal interview, 12 October 1973.

Garcia, Mary R. Parent Coordinator, Tulare Elementary School District, Tulare, California. Personal interview, 31 August 1973.

Garcia, Seneita. Director, Tulare County Child Care Educational Program, Visalia, California. Telephone interview, 28 September 1973.

Gomes, Thelma. Assistant Superintendent, Tulare Elementary School District, Tulare, California. Personal interview, 31 August 1973.

Masonhall, Ellis. Director of Guidance, Selma High School, Selma, California. Personal interview, 9 October 1973.

Misquez, William. Bureau of Community Services and Migrant Education, Division of Compensatory Education, California State Department of Education. Personal interview, 29 August 1973.

O'Neil, Ralph. School Psychologist, Novato, California. Personal interview, 20 July 1973.

Riles, Wilson. Superintendent of Public Instruction. State of California, Sacramento, California. Personal interview, 17 October 1973.

Snow, Larry. Principal, Lafayette School, Highland Park, New Jersey. Personal interview, 21 July 1973.

Willett, Mansel J. Consultant, Fresno County Department of Education, Fresno, California. Telephone interview, 19 October 1973.

V. Unpublished Materials

California State Department of Education, Bureau of Elementary and Secondary Education. "Source of Assistance for Junior High, Intermediate, and Middle School Administrators." Sacramento, California, 1972. (Mimeographed.)

Fresno County Department of Education. "Aides." Fresno, California, 1971. (Mimeographed.)

Grant, Albert. "Hypothesis Regarding Parent Participation in the Work of the School." Ed. D. dissertation, Stanford University, 1957.

Irving, Eugene Richard. "Attitudes of Parents and Teachers Toward Pre-School Reading Instruction Initiated by Parents." Ed. D. dissertation, University of Illinois, 1965.

Los Angeles City Schools. "School Volunteer Program Offers New Series of Training Class." Los Angeles, 1973. (Mimeographed.)

Moler, James Milton. "A Study of Good Parent Participation in Elementary Schools." Ed. D. dissertation, University of Virginia, quoted in University Microfilms Inc. *Disserta-*

SOURCES CONSULTED

tion Abstracts, Volume XIX, Number 4, Ann Arbor, Michigan, October, 1958.

Niedermeyer, Fred C. "Effects of School-to-Home Feedback and Parent Accountability on Kindergarten Reading Performance, Parent Participation and Pupil Attitude." Ed. D. dissertation, University of California, Los Angeles, 1969.

Ryan, Elizabeth McIntyre. "A Comparative Study of the Reading Achievement of Second Grade Pupils in Programs Characterized by a Contrasting Degree of Parent Participation." Ed. D. dissertation, Indiana University, 1964, quoted in University Microfilms Inc. *Dissertation Abstracts*, Volume XXV, Number 9, Ann Arbor, Michigan, March, 1965.

Schiff, Herbert Jerome. "The Effect of Personal Contactual Relationships on Parents' Attitudes Toward and Participation in Local School Affairs." Ed. D. dissertation, Northwestern University, 1963, quoted in University Microfilms Inc. *Dissertation Abstracts*, Volume XXV, Number 1, Ann Arbor, Michigan, July, 1964.

Selma Unified School District. "Aid to Families with Dependent Children List: 1972-1973." Selma, California, 1972. (Mimeographed.)

Selma Unified School District. "Report of the Citizens' Community Congress on Education." Selma, California, 1974. (Mimeographed.)

Selma Unified School District. "Application for Funds for Educational Programs." Selma, California, 1973. (Mimeographed.)

Selma Unified School District. "Board of Trustees, Selma Unified School District, Minutes of October 9, 1973, Meeting." Selma, California, 1973. (Mimeographed.)

Selma Unified School District. "Elementary and Secondary School Civil Rights Survey." Selma, California, Fall, 1972. (Mimeographed.)

Selma Unified School District. "Ethnic Survey." Selma, California, 1972. (Mimeographed.)

Selma Unified School District. "Stull Bill Project." Selma, California, 1973. (Mimeographed.)

Stabler, M. Louise. "The Effect of Parental Involvement on the Reading Achievement and Attitudes Toward Reading of Children Who Are Receiving Additional Help in Reading Beyond the Regular Classroom." Ed. D. dissertation, Lehigh University, 1969.

Tulare County Child Care Educational Program. "Parent Involvement Manual." Visalia, California, 1973. (Mimeographed.)

Tulare Elementary School District. "Title I Evaluation: 1972-1973." Tulare, California, 1973. (Mimeographed.)

VI. Newspaper Articles

"Adult Tutor Program a Success." *The San Diego Union*, 4 January 1973.

"After Three Years Riles Sees Education Pledges Fulfilled." *The Fresno Bee*, 2 October 1973, sec. A, p. 5.

"Early Childhood Education—Special Program Continuing." *The Selma Enterprise*, 19 December 1974, p. 11.

"Head Start Parents Seek Greater Education Role." *The Fresno Bee*, 4 November 1973, sec. B, p. 2.

"People Who Help Make Schools Go." *San Francisco Chronicle*, 17 September 1973, sec. A, p. 3.

"Riles: Early School Plan a Success." *The Fresno Bee*, 13 November 1974, sec. A, p. 8.

"Washington School—Still Teaching Basics." *The Selma Enterprise*, 12 December 1974, p. 14.

VII. Other

KMJ T. V., Channel 24, "News," 7 November 1973, "Fresno City Schools Use of Cross-Age Tutors," Mike Hartman.

Index

Achievement: reading, 14, 15; test scores, 11
Advisory committee, 20
Attendance, 15; home calls, 47; irregular volunteer, 39, 49; records, 18, 46, 47; school, 26; telephoning, 47
Attendance Clerk Job Description (Item 14), 70
Attitudes: parents, 14
Audio visual materials: ordering, 25; organizing, 25; preparation, 46; repairing, 25, training, 51
Behavior problems, 15
Bilingual parent volunteers, 29
Books: card catalog, 47; checking out, 47; check-out cards 47; displays, 47; inventory, 47; listing, 17, 47; ordering, 25; organizing, 25; pasting, 25; repairing, 17, 25, 47; reshelving, 25; shelving, 17, 47; stamping, 47
Budget, 20
Cafeteria: parent assistant, 18
Child care, 26
Clerical-technical volunteer duties, 46, 47
Correcting papers, 25, 46
Costume construction, 45
Court decisions, 19
Curricula, 14
Definition of terms, 20

111

Douglas, 11
Duplicating materials, 25, 47
Economic stringency, 13
Educational benefits, 12
Effectiveness of program, 16
Elementary and Secondary Education Act, 15
English as a second language, 46
Enrichment lessons or activities, 24, 84; definition, 29
Environment, 11, 22
Evaluation, 16; definition, 82; program, 39; re-evaluation, 30; student performance, 37
Evaluation Interview (Item 25), 85, 91
Expenditures, 20
Federal philosophy, 15, 16
Feminine gender, 10
Field test, 10
Field trip, 25, 48, 51
Filing, 25; picture, 46; volunteer, 49
Financial considerations, 19
Fine collections, 17, 47
Foundation grants, 19
Games, 46
General Education Provisions Act, 16
Goals, 23, 24, 35, 36, 37, 39, 50, 82; definition, 27; re-evaluation, 30; selection, 27
Grounds Supervisor Job Description (Item 15), 71
Health: clearance, 50; office, 47; problems, 26
Health Assistant Job Description (Item 16), 72
Human potential and resources, 12
Implementation phase, 51
Independent learning projects, 25
Individualized instruction, 24, 28, 29. 37, 84; defination, 20

Information Leaflet - English (Item 9), 42, 64
Information Leaflet - Spanish (Item 10), 42, 65
Inquires, 23, 30; parent, 26, 33, 34; staff, 24, 31, 32, 37
Instructional volunteer duties, 46
Insurance policies, 19
Intelligence, 11, 13
Interview, 18; evaluation, 82, 85; individual, 24, 37; newspaper reporter, 42; volunteer screening, 45, 48
Inventory, 17, 47
Kennedy, 35
Language limitations, 26
Large group volunteer assistance, 46
Learning material construction, 25
Learning tasks, 20
Legal implications, 18
Legislation, 14, 15, 19
Letter, cover (Item 23), 83, 89
Librarian, 39; guide book, 36
Library (Media-Center), 12, 17, 21, 25, 38, 46, 51
Library Assistant Job Description (Item 12), 68
Library Publications (Item 7), 38, 52, 61, 62
Local funds, 19
Lunch: count, 18, 47; duty, 25; money, 47; supervision, 47
Minorities, 17
Moler, 14
Morale, 14
Motivation: children, 18, 25, 29, 85; student, 12, 83
Multi-cultural center, 17
Music lessons, 48
National Education Association, 51
Need: assurance for children, 54;

INDEX

parent volunteer programs, 9; parent volunteers, 17; social, 14
Non-English speaking students, 24, 29, 84, 85
Nurse, 25
Objectives, 23, 24, 27, 37, 38, 50, 82, 83, 85; definition, 27; rating scale, 28; re-evaluation, 30; selection, 27
Observed Results (Item 22), 27, 83, 85, 87
Office: display, 48; school, 18
Orientation for Parent Volunteers (Item 19), 52, 75, 76, 77, 78
Orientation Information for Parent Volunteer Supervisors (Item 4), 37, 56, 57
Orienting volunteers, 39; definition, 50; programs, 50
Paid volunteers, 19
Parent: orientation, 37; participation, definition, 21; satisfaction, 12; tea, 17, 43; training, 37; volunteer, definition, 21
Parent Coordinator, 38, 39; duties, 39, 40; interview, 40; qualifications, 39; volunteer interview, 48
Parent Coordinator Job Description (Item 8), 39, 63
Parent Inquiry (Item 2), 26, 33, 34
Parental interest, 15
Parent-Teachers Association at Washington School, 27, 41
Partnership, cooperative, 35
Pertinent research, 13
Placing volunteers, 44, 45-50
Planning, 15, 24, 37
Playground: duty, 25; supervision, 47
Plays, skits, 48

Policies: guide book, 36, 37
Policy decisions, 16
Procedures manual, 36, 37
Program, design, 39; developing, 16; participants, definition, 121
Program Guide No. 44, 15
Public relations, 14; approaches, 41, 42; newspaper article, 42, purposes, 40, 41; radio announcement, 43
Publicity, 14
Questionnaires (See Inquiries)
Rating scale, 28
Ratio: adult/student, 12
Reading: achievement tests, 14, 15, 46; aloud, 25
Recognizing volunteer service, 53, 54
Recording grades, 25
Reimbursement, 19, 20
Relationships: adult-student, 54; community/school, 12, 18; family/school, 12; home-community, 28; home/community-school, 24, 83; staff and parent, 37; student/school, 12
Remuneration, 19
Repair: school facilities, 48
Resource teacher: definition, 21
Riles, 12
Ryan, 14
Savings: monetary, 12
Schiff, 14
School Parent Volunteer Program: definition, 21
Screening volunteers, 44
Secretarial Assistant Job Description (Item 13), 69
Secretary, 18, 25
Sewing: costumes, 26
Slides: arrange, 25; presentation, 25
Small groups, 18, 25, 46
Socioeconomic factors, 12
Soliciting suggestions, 24

Staff: coordinator, 38; definition, 21; development workshop, 37; meeting, 37; orientation, 36, 39
Staff Inquiry (Item 1), 24, 31, 32
Story telling, 25, 46
Student Handout (Item 24), 27, 83, 90
Study habits, 15
Suggestions: parent, 27; staff, 24
Supervision: halls, 47, buses, 47
Supervisor: definition, 21
Supervisor Evaluation of the Volunteer (Item 26), 86, 92
Tape recording, 25
Team approach, 22
Test: diagnostic, 20, 46; word meaning, 14
Title I, 15; activities, 15; development, 16; evaluation, 16; operation, 16; planning, 15
Training volunteers, 36, 39, 41; credit, 51; definition, 50; on the job, 52, 53; techniques, 51
Translating: notices, 47; parent conferences, 47
Tutoring, 25, 46
Typing, 18, 25, 47
U.S. Department of Health, Education and Welfare, 16; Office of Child Development, 16
U.S. Office of Education, 15
Very Important Parent Award (Item 21), 54, 81
Visual aids, 18; construction, 45
Volunteer duties, 24, 25, 46-48
Volunteer: bilingual, 25; recruitment, 39, 40, 41; salary, 20; schedule, 49
Volunteer Attendance Record (Item 5), 37, 59
Volunteer Information (Item 6), 27, 37, 60, 83, 84
Volunteer Questionnaire (Item 11), 48, 66, 67
Volunteer Record (Item 17), 39, 49, 73
Volunteer Record - Special Programs and Activities (Item 18), 49, 74
Volunteer Self-Evaluation (Item 20), 53, 79, 80